PENGUIN BOOKS

MARINA TSVETAYEVA

Elaine Feinstein is a poet and novelist. Her many novels include *The Border* and *Mother's Girl*; *Badlands* is her latest collection of poems. She has written a full-scale biography of Marina Tsvetayeva entitled *The Captive Lion* and has translated and edited the *Selected Poems of Marina Tsvetayeva*. She has written the volume on Bessie Smith in the Lives of Modern Women series and is currently working on a new collection of poems.

LIVES OF MODERN WOMEN

General Editor: Emma Tennant

Lives of Modern Women is a series of short biographical portraits by distinguished writers of women whose ideas, struggles and creative talents have made a significant contribution to the way we think and live now.

It is hoped that both the fascination of comparing the aims, ideals, set-backs and achievements of those who confronted and contributed to a world in transition and the high qualities of writing and insight will encourage the reader to delve further into the lives and work of some of this century's most extraordinary and necessary women.

Titles published in this series

Elaine Feinstein

Marina
Tsvetayeva

Penguin Books

PENGUIN BOOKS

Published by the Penguin Group
27 Wrights Lane, London W8 5TZ, England
Viking Penguin Inc., 40 West 23rd Street, New York, New York 10010, USA
Penguin Books Australia Ltd, Ringwood, Victoria, Australia
Penguin Books Canada Ltd, 2801 John Street, Markham, Ontario, Canada L3R 1B4
Penguin Books (NZ) Ltd, 182–190 Wairau Road, Auckland 10, New Zealand

Penguin Books Ltd, Registered Offices: Harmondsworth, Middlesex, England

First published 1989
10 9 8 7 6 5 4 3 2 1

Made and printed in Great Britain by
Richard Clay Ltd, Bungay, Suffolk
Set in Monophoto Photina

CONTENTS

LIST OF ILLUSTRATIONS

Marina with her son Georgy Efron at Clamart, 1933. (Ardis
  Publishers)

Sergei Efron in Paris, 1937. (Ardis Publishers)

Marina Tsvetayeva in the 1940s in the Soviet Union. (Ardis
  Publishers)

CHRONOLOGY

1928	Mayakovsky visits Paris.
1932	Sergei joins Communist front organization.
1935	Pasternak visits Paris for Congress of Writers.
1937	Alya returns to Russia.
	Murder of Ignace Reiss: Sergei flees to Russia.
1938	Invasion of Czechoslovakia.
	Poems for Chechia.
1939	*The Bus.*
	Tsvetayeva returns to Russia.
	Alya is arrested.
	Sergei is imprisoned.
1941	Germany invades Russia.
1941	Tsvetayeva hangs herself in Yelabuga.

ACKNOWLEDGEMENTS

I would like to record with gratitude my debt to Angela Livingstone, University of Essex; Simon Franklin and Jana Howlett, University of Cambridge; Richard Davies, Librarian of Leeds University Russian Archive; Patrick Miles; and Bernard Comrie, whose help made the translation of *Selected Poems of Marina Tsvetayeva* and the writing of *A Captive Lion* possible. I am also grateful to Yevgeny Yevtushenko, Margarita Aliger and Viktoria Schweitzer, who made much of my early research possible. I would also like to thank Maria Enzensberger and Annie Lee for their generous assistance in preparing this volume for press.

E.F.

Tsvetayeva's spirit is not easily caught in photographs. Her gestures are remembered more than her features: her incessant smoking, her loose-limbed gait, the movements of her boyish figure. She herself thought that her appearance was irrelevant. She had none of the grandeur of a woman who is beautiful, or who exacts the kind of devoted service that Anna Akhmatova was able to command. Yet the changeability of her face from day to day was itself a mark of resilience. She had no strong bones to support an impassive face; every change of mood showed on it. Hers was often the face of a driven creature, sometimes an impatient one, but never (except in the posed 'pretty' photographs of the early 1920s) static. She could look weary, standing on the cobbles of Clamart one day in 1933, staring towards her son with her hair unkempt and her dress like that of a poor gypsy; and then appear ten years younger at the seaside in the summer of 1935, her hair loose and longer, and sunlight erasing the harsh lines from nose to mouth.

Poets have often attracted devoted servants to protect

their unworldliness. Far from finding any such fortune, Tsvetayeva found herself in harness most of her life to the needs of a sick husband and the support of her family. For most of her married life she had to work while coping with conditions of unremitting poverty, for which her comfortable childhood had provided little preparation. For all her vitality, she came to accept without bitterness the role of worshipper rather than beloved; perhaps she chose it. Her impracticality often looked like self-indulgence to fellow *émigrés*, because they did not grasp the enormity of her struggle.

She was not a ruthless woman, though her daughter's portrait of her in her six-year-old journal strikes a certain chill.

MY MOTHER

My mother is very strange.

My mother is not at all like a mother. Mothers always admire their child and children generally, but Marina does not like little children. She has light brown hair; it curls up at the sides. She has green eyes, a hooked nose and pink lips. She has a slender build and arms which I like. She is sad, quick and loves Poems and Music. She writes poems. She is patient and tolerant to the extreme. Even though she gets angry she is loving. She is always hurrying somewhere. She has a big heart. A gentle voice. A fast walk. Marina's hands are full of rings. Marina reads at night. Her eyes are nearly always full of fun. She does not like being pestered with silly questions, then she gets very angry.

Sometimes she walks about like someone lost, but then she suddenly seems to wake up, starts to talk and again seems to go off somewhere.[1]

Yet far more than most poets, she accepted her responsibilities without self-pity. When, in a letter, Tsvetayeva rebuked Boris Pasternak for travelling back to Russia without visiting his mother, she added incredulously: 'Among you superhumans I was *merely* a human ... I have only ever been myself (my soul) in my notebooks and on solitary roads (which have been rare), for all my life I have been leading a child by the hand.'[2] Among those children, she might well have included her own husband. When she first heard *Eugene Onegin* read aloud as a child, she longed for a love equally devouring and intense. It was a need that, as Mark Slonim observed, made her friendship like meeting 'a single naked soul', and it was largely thwarted.

By 1926 she had begun to ask proudly what she still hoped for in her relationships with men. Her analysis was grim, as she probed for an understanding of the reasons why she had never inspired the kind of passion she longed for. As a sex, she sensed, men preferred Eve to Psyche, and for all her power to fascinate, she had never found anyone to love her more than anything else in the world. This was not only because she was too spiritual, but because there was something in her that made her more of a guest than a host.

People shoot themselves for the mistress of the house, not a guest ... I do not doubt that I shall be the most prominent woman in the senile memoirs of my young friends – but I never counted in the masculine present.[3]

Always sustained by correspondence with great spirits,

she could rarely number them among her daily acquaintance, and though she always needed the company of fellow poets, there was something inevitable about the antagonism she aroused. However strongly she opposed the Communist regime, she always remained loyal to the greatness of poets in the Soviet Union. For Tsvetayeva, the true poet could have no interest in ideologies. She saw the condition of creation as a visitation analogous to dreaming, when suddenly 'obeying an unknown necessity, you set fire to the house or push your friend down the mountain top'.[4] In the political context of the thirties, that lofty apprehension was altogether misunderstood.

Tsvetayeva's whole life proved to be an inexorable movement into isolation at the peripheries – from Moscow into exile, then from city to outer suburbs, where the drudgery of everyday life became all the more difficult to bear for being so far from the centre of things. It was a sense of the danger of such situations to her psychological survival that made her so desperate not to be isolated in a village outside Moscow when she returned to the Soviet Union. And it makes even more poignant her ultimate loneliness in the small town of Yelabuga, where she took her own life in 1941.

There is nothing like Tsvetayeva in English. It is a matter not only of the violence of her emotions, or the ferocity of her expression. She fulfilled the demands of her 'golden, incomparable' genius (as Pasternak declared her to be) against all the demands of womanhood. In this brief portrait, I wanted above all to honour the stamina that sustained her achievement.

MARINA TSVETAYEVA

Marina Ivanovna Tsvetayeva was born on 26 September 1892 into a household dominated by women. Her father, Professor I. V. Tsvetayev, was forty-five, often away, and absent-minded when at home. The most profound influence on Marina's childhood was that of her mother, his much younger second wife, Maria Alexandrovna. Many years after her mother's death, Marina was to declare that she owed her everything. And certainly it is easy to recognize the lonely courage and pride she absorbed from her mother. Probably the only relief she was to find from her, throughout her formative years, was offered by her half-sister, Valeria.

Maria Alexandrovna herself married without romantic hopes. Tsvetayev was a greying, stooped widower whose former wife (and mother of his two children) had been dead less than a year. In marrying him, Maria Alexandrovna had looked only for some understanding and affection, since the man she loved was estranged from a wife who refused to divorce him. Tsvetayev's first wife, Varvara Dmitrievna, however, had been a woman of exceptional beauty and he continued to love her deeply. She had once studied singing in Naples, and love of music must have seemed a resemblance between the two women, but Varvara Dmitrievna had a light, bird-like gift, where Maria Alexandrovna was an outstanding pianist whose talent was far more than a domestic accomplishment.

For all Professor Tsvetayev's interest in the arts, he was not sensitive to his new wife's feelings, as may be seen in the commissioning of an artist to paint a portrait of his dead wife. Maria Alexandrovna sadly reproached herself in her diary for jealousy: 'Jealous of whom? Of the poor bones in the cemetery?' Yet jealous she was, and quite soon deeply unhappy. When the portrait was completed it was hung high on the white-and-gold-papered wall of the drawing room, where it filled the room with the presence of dead beauty. The house itself had been part of Varvara Dmitrievna's dowry: a one-storey wooden house at No. 8, Street of the Three Ponds, in Moscow.

Maria Alexandrovna found her husband's temperament oppressive and was unhappy to find that he had no ear for music. She also found it difficult to cope with the resentment of her stepdaughter Valeria, who at nine was only twelve years younger than she was. (The son of the first marriage, Andrei, adjusted more easily.) For all these reasons, all her need for love focused upon her first child.

Although she had very much wanted a son, she turned her passionate attention to the education of her daughter Marina for the rest of her short life. The child responded with precocious intelligence. At four, Marina was shown a picture that hung in her mother's bedroom and recorded the duel in which Pushkin was killed by d'Anthès. Her mother never explained to her that the cause of the duel had been Pushkin's wife, the famous beauty Goncharova; the child transposed the duel into a myth with only two figures, the poet and his murderer. It was as if the black and white picture flowed out into her mother's bedroom, which held not a hint of colour in Marina's recollection. There was only a black and white window and the trees outside, her mother, and the terrifying snowy picture on the wall. All the pictures that Marina remembered from the 'House of the Three Ponds' (two murders and one apparition) were in some way threatening. They were to be, as Marina herself put it forty years later, 'an excellent preparation for the terrible century'[5] that awaited her.

Marina soon understood that she was different from other children, and would be judged by different standards. Unlike her younger sister, Anastasia, she was expected to excel in every way; to understand that everyday life was opposed to all that was sacred; and to accept that all talents came from God. At the same time, few practical duties were demanded. A mixture of privilege and exceptional pressure lay behind Marina's unworldliness in later years.

Maria Alexandrovna had no wish to turn her daughter into a poet. On the contrary, she intended to turn her into the concert pianist she had failed to become herself, and her ruthless training at the piano remained one of Marina's most bitter memories of childhood. Although Marina practised every day for two hours, without complaining, her mother saw easily enough that she lacked her own enthusiasm. The knowledge disappointed but did not deter her. She blamed Marina for it. Her next child, Anastasia (Asya), born two years later, escaped all these pressures. This Marina resented. Only *she* needed to excel, it seemed; Anastasia was given love without any such requirement. It was an injustice that complicated the relationship between the sisters. Anastasia admired her sister and followed her lead in everything, but Marina was always impatient with her and sometimes malicious.

For all her mother's bullying, Marina loved the music she heard when her mother went to the piano. She particularly liked sitting with her sister underneath the piano, as if underwater, as the music poured over them, with pots of palms and philodendrons reflected in the polished wood of the piano as if in a black lake. Alongside Marina's understanding of her mother's love for the piano was her grasp of the connection between art and worship. She learned to see the piano as a sacred object, on which nothing should be placed – certainly not newspapers. Maria Alexandrovna made that clear with the persistence of a martyr, every morning, without saying a word, when Marina's father invariably and innocently put them there.[6]

Marina had almost all her early tuition from her mother, and though she was also instructed by governesses, both they and the nannies who looked after her in other ways were displaced by the central importance Marina attached to her mother.

At six, Marina was sent to the Moscow music school of Madame Zograf-Plaksina. She had a firm, rounded face, though it was already possible to detect an obstinacy about the set of her mouth that was missing from her sister Anastasia's expression. (Of the two sisters, it was Anastasia who had inherited the narrow face and sharp features of their mother.) Marina was also a tough child physically, able to take on her half-brother Andrei even though he was two years older than she was.

The intensity of her mother's attention had many pathological elements. It was rare for Marina to earn praise. Her mother seemed angry to discover how much sharper Marina was than the other children. 'And why is it always *you* who knows, when I am reading to *all of you?*' When she detected in Marina a natural passion for literature, she forbade her reading of adult books, and with inexcusable cruelty ridiculed the first poems Marina brought to show her. As a result, an illicit compact grew up between Marina and Valeria, as much from the older girl's feud with her stepmother as from affection between the half-sisters. In this way Marina had access to Gogol's *Dead Souls*, and eagerly devoured Pushkin's *The Gipsies*. In Valeria's room was the whole tree of knowledge: a book cabinet of forbidden fruits, all the sweeter for being under prohibition. A world, too, of female sexuality lay under Valeria's green Venetian mirror: cosmetics and silver pills against menstrual pain suggested bewitching secrets. An erotic version of a childhood devil, ambiguously sexed, and suggesting all the powerful forces of the instinctual world denied by Marina's mother, always appeared in

Marina's imagination in her half-sister Valeria's bedroom. Marina's later attachments to women may well have their source in this childhood alliance.

Other tensions arose from the personality of D. I. Ilovaisky, Valeria and Andrei's grandfather, an alarming man of extremely reactionary beliefs, for whom hatred of the Jews was a particular passion. Remembering his house near Old St Pimen's church on Little Dmitry Street many years later, Marina wrote of a place where 'Everything died out except death. Except old age. Everything: beauty, youth, wonder, life.'[7] Ironically, it was from this side of her extended family that she was to receive her first encouragement to go on writing, from Sergei Ilovaisky, the historian's young son.

Ilovaisky was a harsh man in more than his political beliefs. The tuberculosis that infected, and finally killed, all of his children did not touch him; he kept a cold house, with open windows, and refused to take a horse and carriage anywhere, even as he aged. There was something monstrous in his longevity. When he arrived at the Tsvetayev household, he brought gold coins for Andrei only. He had no interest either in girls or in the children of Tsvetayev's second wife, never even bothering to distinguish their faces sufficiently to name them correctly. Maria Alexandrovna took the coins gravely away and gave them to her stepson. But as she took them, she insisted that his hands should be scrubbed. Although she never discussed the Ilovaisky way of life with her children, the inhuman coldness of it appalled her. She disliked the old man's hatred of all minorities. She was conscious of her own German roots (her family were

Baltic German through her father), loved Heinrich Heine, and admired Rubinstein. This understanding Marina drew from her mother, along with a love for the richness of the German language.

Marina's grandfather, Alexander Danilovich Mein, in contrast, was a jolly, bustling man who brought presents whenever he visited the Tsvetayev household. His background, that of a wealthy Baltic German, played a significant part in Marina's own development; rather like Mandelstam (a St Petersburg Jew), she could have written of being 'in seriousness and honour in the West from an alien family'.[8]

Maria Alexandrovna allowed her daughter to share only one pleasure – a passion for playing with language. In this way, Marina learned to read and write German almost as early as Russian. Whatever her mother questioned her about, Marina in answering looked for rhymes, as if there were a mystical significance in the way one word rhymed with another; and her mother responded gravely, querying the precision of the rhyme, but understanding the premise. The child worked on word associations rather than etymology; when asked for the meaning of 'red carbuncle', she hit on 'red bottle', because of the resemblance to *Karaffe*, and *funkeln*, and was rewarded by an understanding admission that she was at least close to the meaning. This did not prevent Maria Alexandrovna mocking the six-year-old's passionate response to a recital from Pushkin's *Eugene Onegin*. 'You didn't understand anything in that. Well, what could you understand in it?'[9] Marina sensed that the antagonism sprang from her mother's own unhappiness and envy. Of course, every daughter is a rival, but Maria Alexandrovna's ambitions and desires had been so thwarted that her jealousy was as bitter as a dead woman's jealousy of one still alive, with all the ferocious awareness that the chance to live would not now be hers.

A year after her first child was born, Maria Alexandrovna met the man she had once loved, quite by chance, at a lecture by Professor Tsvetayev. When he asked politely after her health, she replied: 'My daughter is a year old. She is very big and intelligent. I am completely happy.' It was a brave lie for a young woman who had married a middle-aged widower still in love with his dead wife. Tsvetayeva, writing of the incident four decades later, commented: 'Oh God, how that minute she must have hated me, however big and intelligent, because I was not *his* daughter!'[10]

The Tsvetayev family spent summers at Tarusa, a small town on the Oka river, not far from Moscow, in the province of Kaluga. It was a quiet town, surrounded by forests and far from the railway, with broad fields on both sides of the river. During Marina's childhood, most of the houses were single-storey wooden *dachas* with painted fences, and gardens behind them with closely planted apple and cherry trees. In trees and courtyards, roosters, hens, geese and baby chickens scurried everywhere. The Tsvetayev house had a large garden, an old orchard, and fruit that ripened all at once in summer: strawberries, cherries, currants and elderberries. Marina recalled the redness and illicit sweetness of those berries in a story about the 'Kirillovnas', a group of Old Believer nuns who lived in the village and were particularly fond of her. Their fondness took the form of feeding victoria plums to her and her sister as soon as their mother's back was turned. They very well understood that such greed would never be countenanced – Maria Alexandrovna's eyes had made that as clear to them as to the children – yet they went on pouring berries from their colanders into the children's daring, hungry mouths.

Marina remembered with an almost erotic longing the nuns' teasing threat that they were going to take her away to live with them:

'Marina, dear, my beauty, stay with us, you'll be our daughter and live with us in our garden and sing our songs . . .'

'Mama won't let me.'

'But wouldn't you stay otherwise?' Silence.

'Well, of course you wouldn't stay . . . you'd miss your mama. She probably loves you a great deal, doesn't she?' Silence. 'Probably she wouldn't give you away for money either, would she?'

'But we won't even ask her mama – we'll just take her ourselves!' said one of the younger ones. 'We'll take her away and lock her up in our garden, and we won't let anyone in. Then she'll live with us behind the hedge.' (A wild, burning, unfulfillable hope began to glow inside me: would it be soon?)[11]

Although Marina may have wanted to be whisked away from her family, she loved the family *dacha* at Tarusa and the way of life there. She remembered her father in his tussore-silk jacket, her mother in her red handkerchiefs, the yellow bonfire and the river Oka, and indeed the story of the Kirillovna nuns contains a notably genial portrait of Professor Tsvetayev himself, resisting his wife's objections to Marina being allowed to go with the family to watch the hay-making. Maria Alexandrovna couldn't stand any kind of family outing, and feared that the ride behind the horses was likely to make Marina sick. Marina clearly found her father gentler than her mother, although he challenged his wife's opinion only meekly.

Marina inherited a Moscow such as Boris Pasternak was to recall – of cloisters, towers and churches with gold-crowned cupolas. Like Professor Tsvetayev, Leonid Pasternak was a member of the teaching staff of Moscow University's School of Painting, Sculpture and Architecture. His wife Rosalya, like Marina's mother, was a talented pianist. The Pasternak household, however, was wholly different from that of the Tsvetayevs: Leonid and Rosalya were warmly attached to one another, and their Odessa Jewish descent made for a southern ebullience Marina's family notably lacked. Pasternak's earliest memory was of listening to a trio performed by his mother and two professors from the Moscow Conservatory. Marina's family seem to have rarely entertained, since Tsvetayev was not only absent-minded but inturned, and a little stingy. The bare-footed poverty of his childhood as a priest's son in Talitsy is only part of the story: he genuinely disliked spending money. For him, even the purchase of new clothing produced misery and apprehension. That asceticism may well have put down roots in Marina's own spirit. Certainly, the almost reclusive character of her family background stunted Marina, so that she never acquired the easy rapport with others that blessed Boris Pasternak for most of his life, and made his tentative stammer a tic that friends remembered with affection. At the same time, Marina's isolation was a source of later strength. She learned unnaturally early to rely on the habit of self-appraisal that was to sustain her through a loneliness few writers have had to endure.

Unlike Pasternak, whose family hospitality brought Tolstoy, Tchaikovsky, Gorky, Rilke and many others through their drawing room on the way to the artist's studio, Marina's memories of her childhood focus almost exclusively on close members of her family. And her first love was given to Seryozha (Sergei) and Nadya, children of her Ilovaisky relations, who often joined the Tsvetayev family on holidays in Tarusa. At four years old Marina stood for hours in complete silence, immersed in watching Seryozha work away at the slope running from the river Oka to the Tsvetayev *dacha*, digging a stairway into the steep side of the hill. By the time he was seventeen (and Marina only seven), Seryozha knew her well enough to encourage her to copy out her secretly written poems. It was a request that made her shy, but his attention was worth far more to her than he knew, even if it arose mainly from a kindness that sprang from the knowledge that his death was approaching. Both Seryozha and Nadya had already contracted tuberculosis. At first Ilovaisky took them to Spasskoe, where they were fed on a diet of oatmeal and made to sleep with the windows open in a singularly damp climate, but in 1902 he more sensibly took them to Nervi on the Bay of Genoa in Italy.

It was Nadya who aroused Marina's deepest passion; the girl's faint smile, dark eyes and flushed beauty (all so unlike her own solidly healthy face) were features that attracted Marina's most romantic feelings. But both lives were doomed. Seryozha died first; a month later Nadya, too, was borne off in a coffin, through the February snow. It was a crueller death than Seryozha's, for to the end Nadya had continued to hope and pray for life.

With the loss of these two, Marina experienced the extent of her isolation. It was an isolation that made for precocity, as well as a preternatural voracity for books. (She had read Racine, Corneille, Victor Hugo and most of the Russian classics before she was twelve.) It also gave her the wary self-sufficiency of a natural outsider.

At the age of nine, Marina entered the first year of the Gymnasium No. 4 on the Sadovaya, near Kudrinskaya Square. And Maria Alexandrovna played the piano more and more to herself in an empty drawing room. She made no social calls, though sometimes she went to the theatre or to concerts with friends. By the spring of 1902 her health was beginning to fail, and in November of the same year she learned from her doctor that she, too, had tuberculosis. So it was that the family's travels abroad began. Andrei was left in Moscow with his grandfather, but the rest of the family journeyed to Nervi, which Professor Tsvetayev used as a base for sculpture-spotting trips around the country. Marina was hugely excited at the prospect of seeing the sea. She was only ten, but she already loved Pushkin's magnificent praise of its elemental force. However, her romantic hopes were shattered by her first sight of the real thing. Marina had hoped to see the Nervi that she had imagined from the postcards sent back by her sad, much-loved Nadya Ilovaiskya – cards on which the sea appeared a deep, dark blue, with black pines against it and a brightly lit moon standing out against blue-black clouds. That blue darkness was never to be matched in the Nervi that Marina and Anastasia explored with Volodya, the son of the hotel owner.

As the family arrived at Nervi, Maria Alexandrovna suffered a serious tubercular attack and there was no further chance that day for the children to examine the sea any closer. In the morning, ill though she was, Maria Alexandrovna forced herself out of bed and took her seat at the piano. A few minutes later, there was a knock at the door.

'Allow me to introduce myself, Doctor Mangini. And you, if I am not mistaken, are Signora thus-and-such, my future patient?' (He was speaking in halting French.) 'I was passing by and heard your playing. And I must warn you that if you continue like that, you will not only burn yourself out, you will set the entire Pension Russe on fire.'[12]

Apart from making friends with Volodya, the girls also met a group of anarchists, who taught them revolutionary songs. Some openly discussed the penal servitude they had suffered for their opposition to the Tsarist regime.

In 1903 Maria Alexandrovna's health began to deteriorate, and since it was essential for her to go to a sanatorium,

Marina and Anastasia were sent away to boarding school in Lausanne – the Pensionnat de Mademoiselle Lacaze. Marina was not yet eleven, but luckily her command of French was excellent. She was always academically confident, even though she found it difficult to make friends with children her own age, who found her precocity worrying. With older girls, however, she became something of a pet. Monsieur l'Abbé was less pleased with her opposition to the Catholic church, and set himself the task of winning over her lost soul. The children were taken twice to church on Sundays: once to morning Mass, and again at four in the afternoon. This was unlikely to win Marina's complaisance, and she frequently stopped the hand of her less militant sister as it hovered over the collection plate. By the time the girls had been at the school for a few months, however, both were touched enough by the new faith to write letters that Maria Alexandrovna found alarming. She wrote to Tsvetayev: 'It is uncanny how these Catholics bring up children! My children are no longer little girls. They are turning into nuns.'

Professor Tsvetayev was less alarmed, for they were not immediately removed from Mademoiselle Lacaze's, and it was mainly to bring the children closer to their mother that in February 1905 they were moved to another school, this time at Freiburg in the Black Forest: the Brinck boarding school. There conditions were spartan, and 'bad marks' were given for sheets not tucked in tightly enough or a single hair left in a comb.

Aside from the magnificence of the Black Forest landscape, the days at the Brinck boarding school were doleful. The children looked forward desperately to the start of the summer holidays. Marina behaved so badly that she would certainly have been expelled if Professor Tsvetayev had been able to leave Russia. Their mother was, of course, too ill to be disturbed.[13]

Out of all this misery, Marina was to recall only one pleasurable episode: a visit organized for her to meet a princess – the Fürstin von Thurn und Taxis. In later years, Marina discovered that the magical figure who listened so kindly to her spirited account of *Heidi* was a close friend of the poet Rainer Maria Rilke.

In the winter of 1904/5 Maria Alexandrovna's illness worsened considerably, and Tsvetayev moved her to a sanatorium at St Blasien in Switzerland, where she was confined indoors and the girls had little to do. Walks with their father were not sociable, since he preferred to stride ahead, without talking. He could not even share the genuine grief he felt at the illness of his second wife, whom he had come to depend on.

When Maria Alexandrovna decided to return to Russia she insisted on doing most of the packing, although she was very ill; she remained strong enough to help write letters for her husband, which Tsvetayev dictated in Russian and she translated into French.

When the Tsvetayevs arrived in Russia they stayed first in the *dacha* of a certain Dr Weber in Yalta, where among their neighbours was Ekaterina Peskova, the wife of Maxim Gorky. Professor Tsvetayev, however, disapproved of an attachment that rapidly developed between Marina and Vera, the eldest of the Weber daughters, who was rumoured to have revolutionary sympathies. It was the year that workers bearing icons were massacred outside the Tsar's Winter Palace in St Petersburg, and of the revolutionary Lieutenant Piotr Schmidt's execution; it was also the year of the mutiny aboard the Black Sea battleship *Potemkin*. Yet all through the winter of strikes and shootings, Marina's spirit was too much pained by her mother's illness to be much involved.

At the end of March 1906 Maria Alexandrovna had a serious lung haemorrhage, which was the start of her final steep decline. She had to spend most of her time in bed swallowing ice, and for the first time she accepted without any pretence that she was going to die. The family determined to return to Moscow, but never completed the journey. As Marina recorded, many years later:

The last mortal thing, June 1906. We didn't get as far as Moscow, we stopped at the Tarusa station. They had carried Mother from place to place the whole way from Yalta to Tarusa. 'I boarded a passenger train and I'll arrive in a freight,' she joked. Arms lifted and placed her in the tarantass. But she would not allow herself to be carried into the house. She stood up and, refusing support, took those few steps by herself, past where we stood breathless and immobile, from the porch to the piano, unrecognizable and huge after several horizontal months, in a beige travelling duster which she had ordered made up as a cloak so as not to measure the sleeves. 'Well, let's see what I'm still able to do,' she said smiling and it was clear she was saying it to herself. She sat down. Everyone stood. And there from hands already out of practice, but I don't want to name the things yet, that's still the secret I have with her . . .

That was her last playing. Her last words in that newly added porch of fresh pine boards, shaded by that same jasmine, were: 'I only regret music and the sun.'[14]

Maria Alexandrovna's last will and testament bears out strongly her fear that Marina's early revolutionary period might have led her to give her money away to some foolish cause. She left all her money to her daughters with the proviso that they could not touch it until the age of forty. Ironically, the money was lost altogether when the Communists took over Russia.

After her mother's death, Marina abandoned her practice at the piano. At first astonished, her teachers soon accepted that the importance of music in Marina's life had now diminished.

Had her mother lived longer, Marina would certainly have entered the Conservatory and graduated a fair pianist. Since she lacked that wondrous quality of slowly developing genius that took Pasternak through music and philosophy until he reached his destiny as a poet, only on her mother's death was Marina free to emerge early as her true self as she disentangled herself from the love she had felt for her mother.

Thus, the sea, receding, leaves pits behind, at first deep, then getting shallower, then barely damp. Those musical pits, the traces of Mother's seas, stayed in me for good.[15]

TWO

As a child, Marina hated her own unromantically healthy appearance. At fourteen, she was solidly built and tall for her age. To remove the offensive signs of health from her cheeks, she cut down on food and drank vinegar. Her most serious physical weakness lay in her huge green eyes, which were badly myopic; a factor perhaps in her lack of contact with the world about her, since she rarely wore glasses. She lacked the physical beauty of Anna Akhmatova, but she had both vitality and an adventurous spirit which she determined her new Russian boarding school should not curb. Not surprisingly, her wilfulness soon ensured her expulsion.

However, she had enough money in 1908 to decide on a visit abroad to study French literature at a summer course at the Sorbonne. Professor Tsvetayev's acquiescence was won easily. He seemed remarkably lacking in paternal anxiety for his self-willed daughter.

In the summer of 1909 she returned again to Paris and was able to see Sarah Bernhardt on the stage. She was an early key focus for Marina's idolatry. Later that summer

Marina began to translate *L'Aiglon*, attracted to the sad character of Napoleon II. More importantly, she had begun to write remarkable poetry of her own. (Napoleon's words, '*L'imagination gouverne le monde!*', became one of the epigraphs of her first book of poems, *Evening Album*.)

Her translation has been lost, because after she had finished it she discovered that it had already been translated by Schepkin-Kupernik. Marina was so disappointed to discover a rival that she threw all her work to one side when she heard of its existence, a gesture reminiscent of a spoiled, imperious child.

Her first romance was little more than a flirtation. At fifteen, Vladimir Nilender entered Marina's life, through Lev Kobylinsky (better known under the pseudonym of 'Ellis'), with whom he shared lodgings. A graduate student in history at Moscow University, and an enthusiastic admirer of Baudelaire, Ellis gained enormous prestige in Marina's eyes as a friend of Andrei Bely. Unknown to her, Bely was titillated in his turn by Ellis's knowledge of the Tsvetayeva sisters, but their meeting would not have suited Ellis. Both Ellis and Nilender were in love with Marina, but she was more attracted to Nilender, though she found his proposal of marriage alarming. Her sister Asya recalls the evening Nilender and Marina walked the streets of Moscow together, and how Marina returned shivering with cold, and perplexed. Several days passed before Marina declared the outcome. 'It's over. That evening when we went out for a walk together, we said goodbye and now we shall never see each other again.'[16]

Marina's deepest emotions at this time were generated by women. Whoever entered her heart, she began, in a sense, to invent, to endow them with qualities they did not really possess. Yet in the case of Asya Turgeneva, Marina's adoration was shared by many admirers. In Moscow in 1910 there were many legends surrounding the three Turgenev sisters. Andrei Bely himself was in love with Asya; and she held court, her small head held tilting delicately forward, looking as fine as an etching. Marina observed that her tapered fingers perpetually held a cigarette, and that her lovely head seemed always wreathed in a grey cloud of smoke. On one occasion, Nilender himself was present when Marina visited the sisters. Marina guessed that he too was a little in love with Asya: 'It was impossible not to be in love with her.'[17]

Asya spoke little on these visits, and Marina herself was silenced by Asya's incomparable elegance. But once Asya wore a leopard skin across her shoulders, and Marina won her attention by exclaiming that she herself was just such an animal. In return, she received a prolonged and serious gaze, and a comment on her own remarkable green eyes.

Asya had the manner of a courtly young man, and what lay between her and Marina was decidedly more than friendship: more like an infatuation, without sensuality. The two girls had a common wildness and, once conversation had opened, enjoyed their own daring. Marina was now seventeen, with bobbed hair and high heels, and she had taken up smoking. But it was not a love intended to last, and Marina lost Asya soon after, when the latter married Andrei Bely.

Soon after this, Professor Tsvetayev packed his daughter off to Germany. It was in the summer of 1910, and he had more on his mind than the thought of her general discipline. A scandal that involved him had begun to mount, and came close to ruining him. In January 1909 a theft of prints from the Rumyantsev Museum, of which Tsvetayev was director, was discovered when a grand-duke found some of them in a Moscow shop and saw that the museum stamps had not been fully rubbed out. The trail led to Koznov, a friend of the museum curator, Shurov. At this stage, Tsvetayev managed to retrieve three-quarters of the stolen prints. Nevertheless the Minister of Education, Alexander Nikolayevich Schwartz, decided to appoint a special commission of investigation. There was an element of personal enmity in this, a relic of the days when Tsvetayev and Schwartz had been at school together. A check on the museum stocks was made, and several accusations were levelled at Tsvetayev. These criticisms reached the press, and Tsvetayev prepared a long written reply. His plans were cut short when he received a letter from Schwartz ordering him to resign within three days. Tsvetayev refused. In December of the same year (1909) a Senate report followed, declaring that there were no grounds for Tsvetayev's dismissal as director of the Rumyantsev Museum.

The story should have ended there. Early in 1910, however, Shurov ordered a new stock-taking at the museum as a result of statements made by two informers on the museum staff. In March the Senate repeated its rejection of all charges against Tsvetayev, but Shurov sent an aggressive report to the Senate and by May the newspapers were once again commenting on the scandal. Why precisely Marina's old student friend Ellis chose *this* moment to cut some pages out of several books belonging to the museum is by no means clear. Bely thought it a gesture in support of anarchism. Bely's own absent-mindedness led him to believe Ellis had simply forgotten which books were his own. None of the books was particularly rare or valuable. But the matter had by now become a *cause célèbre* in the press, and Professor Tsvetayev was soon relieved of his duties at the museum. He never recovered from the blow, though he bore it with great courage and continued to work dutifully on the setting up of a new museum.

THREE

A volume of Marina's poetry was published at her own
expense in 1910, and contained many poems written when
she was only fifteen. Many of these are preoccupied with
death. Most of the poems are filled with the longing for
some volcanic passion whose pain she was eager to endure
as 'the sweetest of ailments'.

This first volume of poems, *Evening Album*, was sent by
Marina to the poets Bryusov and Voloshin, whom she had
not yet met. Among the poets to notice her at this early age
was Gumilyov, the leader of the Acmeist movement in
Russian poetry, who wrote of her:

Marina Tsvetayeva is inherently talented and inherently original. It does not matter that her book is dedicated to the radiant
memory of Maria Bashkirtseva, that the epigraph is taken from
Rostand, and that the word 'Mama' is almost never absent from
the pages. All this only suggests the young age of the poetess
which is soon confirmed by her own lines of confession. There is
much in this book that is new: the audacious, at times excessive,
intimacy of tone; the new themes such as childhood infatuations;

the spontaneous unthinking delight in the trivial details of every-day life. As one would have thought, all the principal laws of poetry have been instinctively guessed, so that this book is not only a charming book of a young girl's confession but also a book of excellent verse.[18]

Marina must have known that from this moment on, whatever else was to be denied to her, she could walk boldly among poets in the future. And her literary acquaintance began to grow. Max Voloshin himself soon became her friend. He instigated the relationship by calling upon Marina at home, wearing a top hat, his large face framed by a short curling beard. Marina had not yet read the article he had written about *Evening Album*, and he brought it round for her to look at. Marina received his unstinting praise with apparent calm. Voloshin was amazed to find that she was wearing school uniform, and Marina explained that she was indeed still supposed to be attending school, though all she did was write poetry. She and Voloshin went up to the old nursery, a room the size of a ship's cabin, which was papered with gold stars on a red field. Voloshin squeezed his huge bulk into the room and looked over all Marina's icons, particularly the pictures of Napoleon. He scrutinized the narrow couch hemmed in by a writing table. Then, almost as equals, the two of them began to talk about writing, and how to write. Voloshin had a particular talent for drawing out women favoured with the gift of poetry. He was, more-over, particularly kind to those who were 'unbeautiful favour-ites of the gods'. Much later in life, Tsvetayeva was to recall that no one had treated her mature poems with the same attention as that given by the thirty-six-year-old Voloshin to her early verses.[19]

Marina's talent was already becoming celebrated among poets and writers. Through Voloshin she was introduced to Musaget (a literary café and publishing house) and was soon invited to give a reading herself. Marina and her sister Anastasia (Asya) had grown closer with their awakening interest in the opposite sex. Marina not only confided in Asya, she also drew support from her, and because of this she asked Asya to appear with her at the reading. The two of them went on stage in their Gymnasium uniforms and read together standing side by side, Marina with her uncut hair modestly pulled back from her forehead, and Asya with her thicker and shorter hair falling to her shoulders. At the end there was a moment's silence and then the whole hall burst into applause, which the two girls received with awkward bows. Decades later, Asya was to recollect the occasion with pride.

In the autumn of the same year Marina moved out of her mezzanine room, with its golden stars on their dark red sky, into what had once been the maids' room downstairs. She began to keep indoor plants (especially luxurious ones, such as begonias), and acquired a gramophone, from which flowed Schubert's serenades and the music of Glinka.

Eager for adventure as she was at eighteen, Marina talked her father into letting her travel to the Crimea before the end of the school term, and was also to get his agreement for a visit to Voloshin's *dacha* at Koktebel. She also decided to visit Pushkin's Gurzuf – as if she wanted to take in the whole of her Russian heritage in one gulp. Marina wrote to her family from Gurzuf: about the charm of being alone, of moonlit walks and the joy of being by the sea. She also mentioned a Tartar boy who was so attached to her that he followed her everywhere, but it is clear that her own heart was whole. After a month of solitude among the ruins of a fortress there, Marina arrived at Koktebel on 5 May 1911. Voloshin's mother, a remarkable woman who wore her grey hair swept back to reveal the profile of an eagle, greeted Marina in her long white kaftan sewn with silver and blue. Her nickname, 'Pra', came from 'Pramater', meaning 'the mother of these regions'.

Pra, indeed, ran a matriarchal society in Koktebel. The house was the only house on that part of the Black Sea shore, surrounded by a Kimmerian landscape, traditionally supposed to be the home of the Amazons. Max himself delighted in myths and created many of his own about the landscape, the grottoes and the coastline around his home. He also kept dogs, which closely resembled huge wolves. But Koktebel was chiefly notable for the hospitality Max delighted to extend to young writers, and it was there, at Voloshin's *dacha* at Koktebel, that Marina met the man who was to become her husband: Sergei Yakovitch Efron.

They first met on a deserted shore near Koktebel, with the noise of the sea in their ears. The shore was strewn with small pebbles; Marina had been collecting them when Sergei began to help her. He was a slender boy of seventeen, sadly and meekly beautiful, with astonishingly huge eyes. Marina at once sensed in him the enormity of his need to be loved. With an instant reckless decision (often recalled), Marina predicted: 'If this boy finds and gives me a cornelian, I shall marry him.'[20] Sergei found the cornelian immediately. He was the sixth child of nine from an extraordinary family. His mother, Elizaveta Petrovna Durnovo (1855–1910), came of an ancient aristocratic lineage, the only daughter of an army officer who had been adjutant to Tsar Nicholas I. On the other hand, her husband Yakov Constantinovich Efron came from a large and literary Moscow family of Jewish origin, some of whom had been rabbis. Sergei's father had been a student at the Moscow Technical College. Only politics could have brought him and Sergei's mother together. They were both members of a revolutionary party that had as its aim a just reallocation of Russian land.

Sergei's mother was then a beautiful, black-haired girl who appeared at revolutionary meetings dressed in a ball gown and velvet cape, but, however aristocratic her appearance, Elizaveta's political views had been formed under the influence of Kropotkin and she was a member of the First International. She was also extremely courageous. In the early stages of their friendship, Yakov and Elizaveta carried out several acts of terrorism. On 26 February 1877, for example, it was Yakov who with two others assassinated the police agent Reinstein, who had succeeded in penetrating their Moscow organization before being exposed as an *agent provocateur*. At first it was not discovered who was responsible for Reinstein's murder, and in July 1880 Elizaveta was arrested for carrying seditious literature and materials for building an underground printing press. As a result, she was imprisoned in the notorious Peter and Paul fortress. However, she was luckier than many. Although her father was appalled to discover that she had anarchist sympathies (he was himself an unshakeable monarchist), he used his influence to arrange for her to flee abroad, and soon Yakov was able to follow her. There they were married and spent a further seven years; their first three children were born in exile.

When they returned to Russia, most of their friends had been imprisoned or deported. And the daily troubles of the Efron family were increased by the loss of three of the youngest children through illness. Nevertheless, it was a remarkably idealistic family. In the late 1890s Elizaveta began once again to help in printing declarations and manufacturing explosives. Some of the older children joined in, too. In photographs from that period, Elizaveta's face looks grey and tired. Her high narrow forehead had become wrinkled early and there were lines around the corners of her mouth. The grandeur of the days of ball dresses and capes had changed into a worn toughness. There is one photograph of husband and wife together, in which Yakov's face has some of the characteristics that were to mark Sergei. His face is simple, open and defenceless, with very bright clear eyes.

Elizaveta's political activities reached their peak in the Revolution of 1905. In that year, police repression came down upon the family and shattered it. Elizaveta was sent briefly to the Butyrki prison, and Yakov was only able to secure her release by paying a ruinous amount of money raised with the help of his friends. He took his wife abroad; sick and exhausted, she was never to return to Russia. Yakov, too, died in exile. Elizaveta survived her husband's death, but when the youngest of the sons who had followed them into exile fell ill and died, she lost heart altogether. She died the next day, by her own hand.

In 1905 Sergei himself was only twelve. He had taken no direct part in the Revolution, and perhaps resented the way his loving family had been fragmented in its name. When his mother and father had to leave Russia, his entire existence lost its centre. There was no longer a family home. While still an adolescent, he fell ill for the first time with the tuberculosis that was to recur throughout his life. His illness, and the longing for the mother he felt had deserted him, brought him such bitterness and grief that his family thought it wiser to conceal the fact that Elizaveta was dead, which was a serious error of judgement. When Sergei finally discovered the truth, it was too late to mourn in any traditional way.

Such was Sergei's tragic background. In spite of his continuing sadness, he was very much part of the group of young people who went regularly to Koktebel. However, it was only in Marina that he found someone who was able to release him from the lonely misery that had filled him since his early years. Fatally, she enjoyed her role as rescuer.

Through the autumn of 1911 the two of them continued to lead a strange, childish, playful life, even though Marina soon regarded herself as engaged to Sergei. She herself had become not only part of the group but a dominant member of it, and she had also changed her general style of dress and behaviour from her Moscow self. She now looked like a boy. Her hair was tightly curled, and touched with gold by the sun; the skin of her face, neck and legs (which were bare below the knee) was almost black. Marina had once loved high heels in Moscow, but in the Crimea she wore sandals, and *sharovary* – wide boyish trousers of the Turkish style.

When her sister visited her, she explained that Sergei was all the dearer to her because of his close escape from death after hearing of the suicide of his mother. She particularly loved his physical frailty.

Like everyone else, Asya felt Sergei Efron's charm. There is no Russian diminutive for the name Marina, and aside from Asya, nobody looked for one after childhood. However, everyone knew Sergei as Seryozha, a diminutive that followed him throughout his life.

Seryozha and Asya fiancé, Boris, met for the first time at a Crimean railway station. Marina and Seryozha were to journey back to Moscow ahead. The four young people stood on the platform, waiting for the train, while the sisters talked about their father, who had been ordered by his doctors to take a rest at Bad-Neuheim. He was, accordingly, away when Marina and Seryozha returned to the house on Three Ponds Street.

They moved into Marina's family home together. Later they moved in with Seryozha's sisters. And they arranged to be married in January 1912. It was not a marriage that can have pleased her father. She was only nineteen, and quite apart from the anti-Semitism of the Ilovaisky family, there would have been a gaol sentence and a suicide to conceal on the Durnovo side of Seryozha's family. It is quite possible that Marina was already pregnant. In any case, the wedding was celebrated quietly.

FOUR

The only period of shared happiness in Seryozha and
Marina's lives turned out to be the two years between their
first meeting and the start of the First World War. Thanks to
the second wife of Marina's Grandfather Mein, they could
afford to buy a house in the old merchant quarter. Two
years later they decided to move, in order to be more cen-
trally located. They chose a three-bedroom flat at No. 6
Boris and Gleb Street in Old Moscow, a modest apartment in
which they lived without questioning their privileged gaiety.
Marina knew that her happiness with Seryozha depended
on the child-like quality that held them as if they were part
of the same dream.

Seryozha's own talent was to lie in recognizing the greatness of others. He loved to be surrounded by lively and
talented practitioners of all the arts, and it had been no
accident that he and Marina had met at Voloshin's *dacha*.
He was not envious of Marina's genius, because her attention and devotion to him was so unmistakable. In many
ways, his easy charm made him more attractive on first

meeting than Marina, and this was particularly true among actors and actresses. Marina was not exactly shy with them, but their extrovert, non-intellectual company disturbed her and she was piqued by her inability to impress them. Seryozha's easy gaiety made up for that awkwardness. Thus they bolstered one another.

Marina's second book, *Magic Lantern*, was published in 1912. However, for the first time in her life she no longer put writing before everything else, and she no longer even wrote every day. Their first child, a daughter, was born on 5 September 1912. At her christening her godfather was Professor Tsvetayev and her godmother was Voloshin's mother, Pra, and the child was named Ariadne though she was usually called Alya.

In the last years of her father's life, Marina grew closer to him. She dealt with all his correspondence and was delighted when the Tsar, who was to be present at the opening of her father's cherished new Museum of Fine Arts, declared that Professor Tsvetayev was to be awarded the Order of the Guardian of Honour. Both daughters now felt considerable affection for the old man, and together they bought him a splendid silver tray which he grumbled they could not afford. In a memoir written in the 1930s, Marina made gentle fun at his continuing parsimony, which led him to insist on shopping for his daughters' clothes himself, to make sure that the fabric was sufficiently durable. In old age, after obstinately continuing to work on through all his adversities, there was a charm in his unworldliness. On the day of the museum's opening, he was dressed in an old greenish-grey dressing-gown when an old friend called on him to present him with a laurel wreath, which he wore for a moment without any sense of looking comic.

When the Tsvetayev family entered the museum, it was packed with the grand and the distinguished, many wearing medals. Among them, Marina (then pregnant with Alya) and Seryozha seemed strangely young. Politically they were altogether innocent. Seryozha, for all his Jewish and revolutionary inheritance, remained remote from the reforming ferment among the intelligentsia. For Marina, one of the high points of the day was watching the Tsar talking to her father, and she had no qualms about the magnificence of the occasion.

When Marina's father died unexpectedly on 30 August 1913, fifteen months after the opening of the museum, Marina was well provided for. She had never been as passionately attached to her father as she had been to her mother, yet she had always respected both his courage and his wish to serve the visual arts. Now his death left her an orphan, and made her even more eager to draw the bonds between herself and Seryozha closer than before, for reassurance.

By now Marina was looking her most voluptuous: her face full without podginess, her dresses long and rich-fabricked, with many chains and amulets on her plump bosom. She wore stiff silks, deeply cut bodices and long voluminous skirts.

Both Seryozha and his two sisters were pupils at a drama school, and took part in studio performances; the oldest brother, Pyotr, had been a professional actor. Seryozha had some dramatic talent, and he enjoyed his performances on the boards. Marina, who had always had a passion for the theatre, was at first happy enough to join the group. These young people could not have anticipated how short a lease their life of gaiety had left to run.

If they looked ahead, it was by fortune-telling. New Year 1914 opened with just such an occasion at Koktebel. Marina and Seryozha arrived with Asya and Boris, through a snow-storm so alarming that their drivers had been reluctant to risk the journey. They were received into Voloshin's welcom-ing bear-hug. The exhilaration of arriving through such weather gave the evening a special enchantment and they began telling fortunes using Voloshin's Bible, too absorbed in the game to realize that the tower in which they were sitting was on fire until they could actually smell smoke. In later years, Marina recorded a vision of Voloshin lifting his hand towards the flame and uttering words of magical power, while the others rushed more practically to bring buckets of sea water. In her memory of the incident, the fire died out at Voloshin's command. It was not an image that suggested she had much grasp of the events to come.

Seryozha was a student when the war began. He was eager to take part in the fighting. Marina had begun to write obsessionally again, and her writing was growing in confidence. He could not mistake her enormous energy, and he already knew that she had ceased to direct her passion towards her family alone. He was sent initially to the front as a male nurse with an ambulance train. He had tried to persuade several medical boards that he was fit enough for active service, but only his intense determination finally won him admission to an officers' training school, for which he was not particularly suited. A fatal ingredient in his desire to see action was a need to impress Marina.

Marina's life at this time was frenetic and wilful but retained a firm domestic structure. This was partly a question of money. She could afford a nanny to look after Alya, and was well able to run a complicated household in her own peremptory fashion. In her memoir, Alya reported a succession of nannies; one was sacked for taking the small child to the wrong church, and another for having dirty hands. Marina decided everything, including the time when toys had to be put away and when Alya had to go to bed. Walks with Marina were delightful adventures, however, even though she always insisted on Alya being dressed with formal correctness: 'boots, hoods, gaiters, straps, hooks, buttons, *endless* buttons'.

Alya was brought up to speak clearly and coherently at all times, and Marina treated her like an adult almost as soon as she could speak at all. In many ways Marina's behaviour recalled that of her own mother, even to instances of occasional cruelty. When Alya drew her first little man, with arms and legs like sticks and a head like a cabbage, and called her mother to see it, she must have been expecting praise. Instead, Marina pretended to find difficulty in making out any figure at all, and made fun of the matchstick legs and the teeth that resembled a fence. Alya always felt that

Marina's mockery then was more merciless than the occasion seemed to merit.

Marina was determined that no opportunity to form Alya's growing intelligence should be wasted, and took responsibility for every facet of her daughter's development. She taught Alya to read and write herself, as soon as she saw that the child was capable of forming letters. Even a visit to the circus could not be undertaken casually. As a result of this intense personal teaching, Alya continued to hear the voice of her mother inside her head like the voice of conscience for many years afterwards.

In other ways Marina was often an enchanting mother, and rewards for good behaviour were usually gifts of her presence: she would read to Alya from a favourite book or take her for a walk. A visit to her mother's room was a very special privilege. Alya recalls it as a place of enchanted clutter:

... a many-cornered, multi-faceted room, with a magical blue chandelier from the reign of the Empress Elizaveta hanging from the ceiling, and a wolf's skin (rather frightening but fascinating at the same time) by the low divan ... I remember my mother's quick bending down towards me, her face next to mine, the smell of Corsican jasmine, the silken rustle of her dress and the way she would quickly settle down with me on the floor.[21]

At the centre of Marina's privacy, of course, was her writing desk: and there were also many objects that recalled her own childhood. For instance, there was her grandmother's musical box, which played a minuet, and there was also a gramophone on which Marina liked to play gypsy songs that she had first heard sung at a concert. At this time, Marina's interest in gypsies was part of her love of everything exotic. She liked to believe in the Romany gift for telling the future, and she enjoyed their confidence-trickster patter. Some premonitory intuition of her own led her to praise their 'imperial fecklessness' to her young daughter.

Marina's life was once again centred around the love and admiration she felt for the poets she had begun to meet. Few of them were her equals. One of them was Tikhon Churilin, a minor surrealist poet. Their relationship was intense, if not necessarily sexual.* On Marina's side, an infatuation provided excitement without necessarily involving disloyalty to Seryozha. Marina's most passionate erotic involvement in the years between 1914 and 1916, however, was with a woman: Sophia Parnok, best known at the time as a translator of poetry (though she was later to write some remarkable poems of her own), and an unashamed lesbian all through her life. She came from an affluent Jewish family in southern Russia, and the descriptions of her in Marina's poetry suggest an arrogant bearing and handsome, even heavy features – 'Beethoven's face', with eyebrows like a heavy ridge.

The relationship between the two women began immediately after their introduction in October 1914, and continued until February 1916. Marina was very much the

---

* In an autobiographical poem published in *Julistan* in 1916, Churilin dedicated a section called 'Love' to Marina Tsvetayeva.

intoxicated lover throughout, and for once, sensuality rather than infatuation was the key to the relationship: Sophia understood how to give Marina a deeper sexual pleasure than she had yet experienced.

Marina made no attempt to hide her love affair, and the two women began travelling around Russia, staying occasionally at places of historic interest and making love wherever they slept. Not surprisingly, Seryozha found not only the affair but also the attendant gossip bitterly humiliating, perhaps all the more so since Marina's emotional attachment was far from equally reciprocated, Sophia Parnok never feeling the slightest compunction in taking up with other women. Part of his determination to join in the war undoubtedly came from his wish to escape from the pain of the situation. In spite of her new relationship, Marina continued to feel as if she still belonged to him in some other, more enduring way. She wrote as much every day, felt his suffering like a burden upon her heart, and insisted that she 'loved Sergei for life'.

It is, however, the love for Sophia Parnok that occasioned the following strange and beautiful poem:

> We shall not escape Hell, my passionate
> sisters, we shall drink black resins –
> we who sang our praises to the Lord
> with every one of our sinews, even the finest,
>
> we did not lean over cradles or
> spinning wheels at night, and now we are
> carried off by an unsteady boat
> under the skirts of a sleeveless cloak,

we dressed every morning in
fine Chinese silk, and we would
sing our paradisal songs at
the fire or the robbers' camp,

slovenly needlewomen (all
our sewing came apart), dancers,
players upon pipes: we have been
the queens   of the whole world

first scarcely covered by rags,
then with constellations in our hair, in
gaol and at feasts
we have bartered away heaven

in starry nights, in the apple
orchards of Paradise.
– Gentle girls, my beloved sisters,
we shall certainly find ourselves in Hell.[22]

Love between women was not in fact thought of as especially sinful in the society in which Marina usually moved. Her true guilt came from the pain she knew she was causing Seryozha, the more painful as her relationship with Sophia deteriorated. In January 1916, she discovered another woman in Sophia's bed. Even if Marina had been willing to accept that blow to her pride, Sophia made it impossible for her by declaring that their love affair was at an end. Months of unforgiving hatred followed in Marina's heart.

Years later, Marina described her rejection by Parnok as

the first catastrophe of her life. At soirées given by literary and theatrical personalities of the time, however, Marina managed to remain elegant and self-assured; and when she was given the opportunity to give a reading in St Petersburg in January 1916 she was greatly excited, even though it meant parting from her daughter for the first time.

Most of Marina's poetry written between 1915 and the Revolution was published in a literary journal, *Northern Notes*, edited in St Petersburg by a wealthy Jewish couple, Sophia Chatskina and her husband Jacov Saker. Marina refused to take any money from them as fees, but accepted gifts instead; the perfume 'Jasmine de Corse', which Alya remembered, was probably such a present.

Her great wish was that Anna Akhmatova would be in her audience that evening. She was not, but Tsvetayeva still read as though she were. As she was to put it two decades later, she read as if 'to give Moscow to Petersburg as a gift, to give Akhmatova Moscow in myself, in my love, to present it to her and to pay homage'.[23]

Kuzmin* was in the audience, and, more significantly, Mandelstam. Tsvetayeva observed that he had eyes 'like a camel's'. Tsvetayeva's poems were applauded, even though she read a poem against the war and in praise of Germany, in which she swore that she would love Germany to the grave. She also read a poem written the previous year:

---

* Mikhail Alexeevitch Kuzmin (1875–1936), a poet, playwright and composer who had earned some notoriety by writing of love between men.

I know the truth – give up all other truths!
No need for people anywhere on earth to struggle.
Look – it is evening, look, it is nearly night:
What do you speak of, poets, lovers, generals?

The wind is level now, the earth is wet with dew,
the storms of stars in the sky will turn to quiet.
And soon all of us will sleep under the earth, we
who never let each other sleep above it.[24]

Altogether Tsvetayeva was intoxicated by her reception, and she had a joyous sense that contained in the *Northern Notes* offices, with their walls lined with books and dark blue wallpaper and with white bearskins on the floor, was a miraculous new world; one in which, when the telephone rang at two in the morning and a voice inquired, 'Is it too late to come over?' the reply came in the very spirit of Tsvetayeva's own desires: 'Of course not, we're reading poetry.' This exalted state, more than any particular events, helped to heal the wound of rejection by Sophia Parnok and encouraged Marina to open a relationship with Osip Mandelstam.

Shortly after the recital at St Petersburg, Mandelstam began to visit her in Moscow. He also spent part of the early summer of 1916 with her at Alexandrov in Vladimir province, where she was taking a brief holiday to visit her sister Asya. Of the many love affairs with men that Marina embarked upon with such intensity during this period, it was probably the only one that was physically consummated. In the nature of things, it is hard to be sure even about that. Salomea Halpern,* in correspondence with Vera Traill (formerly Suvchinsky) in 1979, remarked, 'I had always assumed Osip and Marina were lovers'; though a few lines later she added, 'Osip and I never discussed these things.'

At the same time, Marina's enjoyment in being with someone so young and finely gifted had a kind of narcissism about it – understandable because both of them clearly felt that being together transcended the ordinary world.

Both poets write of walking about Moscow, smoking and talking together as a sleepless, even sexless, intoxication. It was one of Marina's few relationships with a poet of her own stature that was not to depend largely on correspondence. Nadezhda Mandelstam (Osip's wife), writing (in *Hope Abandoned*) of their friendship, acknowledged that Marina's love stemmed from the finest impulse of her noble woman's soul. What Madame Mandelstam recognized as generosity lay in her lack of possessiveness. Marina treated Mandelstam as a wild creature, and did not even resent the fact that it was Mandelstam who became restless first.

In 1916 Tsvetayeva wrote lyrics for Mandelstam in which she offered him Moscow; she also wrote of their night-time walks. It is not often that poems by two different poets that clearly record the same occasion can be put side by side.

---

* Then the Princess Andronnikova, addressed as 'Solominka' in Mandelstam's poetry.

MARINA TSVETAYEVA

Marina wrote:

> You throw back your head, because
> you are proud. And a braggart.
> This February has
> brought me a gay companion!
>
> Clattering with gold pieces, and
> slowly puffing out smoke, we
> walk like solemn foreigners
> throughout my native city.
>
> And whose attentive hands have
> touched your eyelashes, beautiful boy, and
> when or how many times your
> lips have been kissed
>
> I do not ask. That dream my thirsty
> spirit has conquered. Now
> I can honour in you the
> divine boy, ten years old!
>
> Let us wait by the river that
> rinses the coloured beads of street-lights:
> I shall take you as far as the square
> that has witnessed adolescent tsars.
>
> Whistle out your boyish
> pain, your heart squeezed in your hand.
> My indifferent and crazy creature –
> now set free – goodbye![25]

In the same year, Mandelstam wrote the following poem, later published in *Tristia* (1922):

> With no confidence in miracles of resurrection,
> We wandered through the cemetery.
> Here on earth, you know, ubiquitously
> . . . .
> . . . .
> . . . .*
> Where Russia stops abruptly
> Above the black and god-forsaken sea.
>
> An ample field escapes
> Down these monastic slopes
> I did not want to leave the spacious Vladimir
> To travel south.
> But to stay with that lacklustre nun,
> In the dark [the wooden]
> Village of god's fools,
> Would have been to court disaster
>
> I kiss your sunburned elbow
> and a wax-like patch of forehead –
> Still white, I know,
> Under a strand of dark-complexioned gold,
> I kiss your hand whose bracelet
> leaves a strip of white:
> Touris's ardent summers
> Work such wonders.

* These lines are lost from the surviving Russian version.

How quickly you became a dark one
and came to the Redeemer's meagre icon
And couldn't be torn away from kissing –
You who in Moscow had been the proud one.
Music remains.
A miraculous sound,
Here, take this sand:
I am pouring it from hand to hand.[26]

The sexual element was probably not strong in Mandelstam's attachment. As Marina often complained bitterly, men loved something other than the woman in her. Madame Mandelstam stresses Mandelstam's realization that to stay with such a 'mist-wreathed nun' would have destroyed him. Even allowing for Madame Mandelstam's reasons for jealousy, it was certainly Osip who became bored with the calm landscape of Vladimir province and longed for the Crimea. And it was Marina who continued to insist on their relationship, and to feel proprietorial long after their parting. Many years later, Nadezhda found herself, as a wife, necessarily excluded from their glorious acceptance of one another by Marina's manner. She says justly, 'Though I met Tsvetayeva several times, we never really became friends . . . she was totally intolerant of the wives of her friends.'[27]

Not surprisingly, Marina's new infidelity affected Seryozha painfully. And the physical betrayal was only a part of it. There is one key lyric in the 'Insomnia' sequence in which Marina's excitement in moving alone around streets at night rises to a sense of magical liberation.

In my enormous city – it is night,
as from my sleeping house I go – out,
and people think perhaps I'm a daughter or wife
but in my mind is one thought only – night.

The July wind now sweeps a way for me.
From somewhere, some window, music though faint.
The wind can blow until the dawn today.
In through the fine walls of the breast rib-cave.

Black poplars, windows, filled with light.
Music from high buildings in my hand, a flower.
Look at my steps following nobody.
Look at my shadow, nothing's here of me.

The lights are like threads of golden beads,
in my mouth is the taste of the night leaf.
Liberate me from the bonds of day,
my friends, understand: I'm nothing but your dream.[28]

The beauty of the poem cannot disguise the fact that what was being celebrated was a year of independent adventure, in which no one's feelings but her own mattered. The first ecstatic happiness of her love for her husband had been replaced by something closer to brotherly camaraderie. This did not prevent her from being deeply dependent upon him for emotional support.

Seryozha was away enough to be aware of Marina's behaviour only through gossip, or when she confided in him. He was young, married only four and a half years, and by no means as indifferent to ordinary human jealousy as Marina wished to imagine. Seryozha had always been unusually psychologically dependent on his wife's lover, which had to replace that of a much-loved mother. To his vulnerable, self-distrustful nature, her passions and her problems were equally agonizing.

FIVE

Tsvetayeva was by no means the only writer to find herself untouched by the revolutionary cause – Mandelstam, for instance, did not feel the need to leave his friend's *dacha* in the Crimea, and continued to meditate on the myths of his much-loved Mediterranean. And at the time of the February Revolution of 1917, Marina was in Moscow expecting her second child. The sudden and total collapse of the regime in March left her alarmed at the rioting and none too clear about what was happening. She was not alone in her confusion, though it says little for her political astuteness that she could mistake Kerensky, even briefly, for Bonaparte. The desperation of people who supported the Bolsheviks did not move her, because she could distinguish no single heroic figure among the rebels (unlike Stenka Razin, the legendary bandit whom she had always admired) – only a mob, 'the colour of ashes and sand'. She gave birth to a second daughter, Irina, in April 1917, and understandably hoped above all for civil order. Mandelstam had begun by 1918 to speak of the 'great, clumsy creaking turn of helm'. No such turn was possible for Tsvetayeva, even had she been tempted towards it, while Seryozha was involved with the White cause. Whatever other radical opinions Tsvetayeva may have held, she still saw God and the State united in the Tsar's person. Later on, her hatred of 'all organized violence, no matter in whose name it may be perpetrated or by what name it may be called', gave a moral stature to some lyrics of *Swan's Encampment*,* which otherwise found nobility in a very questionable group of opponents to Bolshevism. One lyric, at least, shows an unerring humanism:

. . .

> On either side, mouths lie
> open and bleeding, and from
> each wound rises a cry:
> – Mother!
>
> One word is all I hear, as
> I stand dazed. From someone
> else's womb into my own:
> – Mother!
>
> They all lie in a row,
> no line between them,
> I recognize that each one was a soldier.
> But which is mine? Which one is another's?

* This has been translated as *The Demesne of Swans* in Robin Kemball's translation of the complete cycle of these poems.

This man was White   now he's become Red.
Blood has reddened him.
This one was Red   now he's become White.
Death has whitened him.

. . .[29]

The chaos of the days following the outbreak of the civil war threw all plans into confusion. Tsvetayeva's own plans involved her crossing Russia four times. In October 1917 she was at Koktebel with Max and Pra. Tsvetayeva eventually included diary notes of those days in her memoir of Voloshin. She heard the news of the Bolshevik victory in Moscow at Max's *dacha*, and on 2 November, on her long journey back towards Moscow, Marina crouched in the corridor of a crowded train, uncertain of what news to believe. News-sheets told of the destruction of Tverskaya Street, the Arbat* and the Metropole hotel. Streets were said to be piled high with corpses. And she did not know whether her own house was standing, or if Seryozha was safe. All her thoughts were for her husband. In the diary that she scribbled on that three-day journey back, she promised: 'If God leaves you among the living, I shall serve you like a dog.' And again: 'I have not once thought of the children. If Seryozha is no more, then nor am I; and nor are they. Alya would not live without me, she wouldn't want to, wouldn't be able to. Like me without Seryozha.' In her imagination, Seryozha was involved, at that very moment, with the last

*A famous old street in central Moscow.

White resistance, and she feared to hear the news of his death.

Moscow was black as she arrived, and guns were still rumbling, but it was possible to take a cab through the almost uninhabited streets even at 5.30 in the morning. At the church of Boris and Gleb she was stopped by a group of guards who would not allow her to enter her own house. Only the interventions of the peasant woman Dunya (who worked for her) sufficed to convince them that she should be allowed in to see her children. When at last she burst in, she found that her fears for Seryozha were exaggerated – he was, in fact, safely in bed – but she still put the urgency of his departure from Moscow before every other consideration. They set off for the Crimea the very same day, leaving the children in Moscow with Seryozha's family, to be collected later. Seryozha's intention was to join the White army re-grouping in the south.

In Tsvetayeva's notes of the time, she recorded:

Moscow, 4 November 1917. In the evening of that same day we leave: S., his friend Goltsev and I for the Crimea. Goltsev manages to collect his officer's pay in the Kremlin (200 roubles). That gesture of the Bolsheviks ought not to be forgotten.

Arrival in a frenzied snow storm in Koktebel. The grey sea. The huge, almost physically searing joy of Max V. at the sight of Seryozha alive. Huge white loaves.

The vision of Max on the bottom steps of the tower, with Thiers on his knees, frying onions. And, while the onions fry, Seryozha and I listen to this recital aloud of Russia's tomorrow, and the day after tomorrow. 'And now, Seryozha, such-and-such will happen . . .' Stealthily, almost rejoicing, like a good sorcerer to children, he gave us in picture after picture, the whole Russian revolution for five years to come: the terror, the civil war, the executions; the barriers; the Vendée; men turned to beasts, the loss of decency, the unleashed spirits of the elements, blood, blood, blood . . .[30]

Marina and Seryozha had wildly misjudged the situation in leaving the children behind. Into the chaos that had begun to engulf Russia, Marina bravely set out again to collect her children. She was lucky even to be able to enter Moscow, while the city was not sealed off by the Red army; leaving again was out of the question. And so it was that Marina and Seryozha were separated and forced to live apart for the next five years.

Seryozha was the single person Marina continued to care about most in the world. The closest relationships Marina formed with men during this period existed mainly to sustain her imagination. Marina needed to be in love in order to feel alive. It was not necessary that those she loved should share her emotion; all that mattered was that Marina could feel strongly.

Pavel Antokolsky (or 'Pavlik' as Marina called him) was a young poet whose verse Marina heard first in 1917, recited by a cadet on the train as she travelled back to Moscow alone. She was so struck by the quality that she sought out the poet herself and invited him to visit her at her flat. There in her kitchen, surrounded by pots and pans, they became friends. Marina, then twenty-five, thought of Pavel as seventeen, the age Seryozha had been when she had first met him; in fact Pavel was twenty-one, but on that first occasion, at least, he seemed a schoolboy. He even wore his school uniform, with the correct buttons, and dressed in it he resembled a little Pushkin with black eyes, the Pushkin of Marina's legend. It was a meeting that Marina described as being 'like an earthquake. Because I understood who he was, just as he understood who I was.' Whether or not Antokolsky was her lover as well as her friend, 'he stayed days, he stayed mornings, he stayed nights . . .' He was himself part of an intense homosexual attachment. The encounter was particularly important because he introduced her to the very centre of the group of young people attached to the celebrated Vakhtangov studio, which was an experimental part of the Moscow Art Theatre – a group of which Marina had been only a peripheral part before.

The theatre seemed like a licensed fairy tale to her, and in that spirit she fell in love with one participant after another. Among these was a young actor from the Vakhtangov studio whom (in her memoirs) she called Volodya. He set the tone of their relationship with his first words: 'You remind me of Georges Sand. She too had children, and she wrote, and she had a hard life in Majorca.'[31] Tsvetayeva was touched by the image he had of her, but the relationship remained a chaste one; although there is something erotic in her description of the pleasure she took in his appearance. It was Volodya, on Holy Saturday 1919, who reached into her loneliness and misery at spending Easter alone with a light, sharp knock at the door. He had come to take them to midnight Mass. It was the night that Volodya himself decided to go and join the White army. Later, when he came to say goodbye, he took a signet ring off his finger and gave it to Marina, who was particularly moved by the gift because she was usually the one to give presents. The afternoon he came to say goodbye, Marina was astonished to see him in daylight for the first time and to observe that his hair was not (as she had imagined) black, but auburn. Volodya was amused at her mistake, saying, 'Marina Ivanovna, I am afraid . . . you always saw all the rest of me in your own way, too. That's why I've always dreaded being in daylight with you. Today you see me blond. Tomorrow you might see me boring. Mightn't it be just as well I'm leaving?'[32] Volodya kissed her forehead and her lips almost ritually, and Marina made the sign of the cross over him three times. He left her with a book about Joan of Arc on which he had written as a dedication: 'You and I love the same things.'

Once again, however, and for all her devotion to Volodya, Marina's most intense attachment during the civil war was to a woman. It was a passion much less sensuous than she had felt for Sophia Parnok, and closer to the loves of her childhood, notably Asya Turgeneva. In those, there had always been a wistful quality; she would so clearly have preferred to be loved as a beauty herself than to celebrate the beauty of others. Yet in her relationship with Sonya Holliday, a half-English actress attached to the Vakhtangov studio, her feelings were clearly returned.

In the winter, Alya and Marina and the baby had to live

downstairs in the warmest and darkest of rooms. In the summer they lived in a long, narrow, attic-like closet with a single window. This room was Marina's favourite, because Seryozha had at one time chosen it for himself. Now it was filled by new voices: argument, conversation, rehearsals and declamations.

Sonya (whose name was always made over affectionately to Sonyechka), was introduced to Marina by Pavlik Antokolsky one evening in 1919. In one of Marina's letters to Anna Teskovà, who was to become a friend in later days in Prague, she wrote that Sonyechka was 'the woman I loved more than anybody else in the world. Simply – she was Love in a woman's form.' She had black plaits, enormous black eyes, and burning cheeks. Marina described her as

A living fire. All of her burns! Cheeks burning, lips burning, eyes burning, white teeth and two black plaits – as though curling in flames – one round her back, the other on her chest. And out of these flames comes a look of such delight, and at the same time much despair! It is as if at the same time she's saying, 'I am frightened! I love!'[33]

On that first occasion, Sonyechka and Marina parted with nothing more than a glance – a questioning, doubting, hesitant glance – but very soon after, Sonyechka telephoned to ask whether she could come and see Marina some time without Pavlik. Marina asked only 'When?'

Marina's reading of her own verse play *Snowstorm* to a studio audience confirmed Sonyechka's wild enthusiasm. Nearly twenty years later, Tsvetayeva could still recall

her exact words: 'Marina, I was so frightened! And afterwards I wept so much! As soon as I saw you, and heard you
– immediately I loved you madly. I understood – it's impossible not to love you madly . . .'[34] There was something
innocent even in the extravagance of Sonyechka's words,
something childish in her style of expression, as there was
in her whole personality. Marina herself said that Sonyechka
could not play any of her adult heroines: 'I had to write of
little girls.' Yet the love she offered was something Marina
looked for in vain in the men she loved for most of her life.
And childish or not, Marina found what Sonyechka said
memorable – for instance, when she explained once how
something had affected her: 'My tears were so enormous –
they were bigger than my eyes!' Marina was so struck by
the poetry of the phrase that she threatened to steal it.
Sonyechka eagerly agreed. 'Do take it, Marina! Take everything you need for your poetry. Take the whole of me!'[35]

This offer must be interpreted only in emotional terms, for
(like Marina herself) Sonyechka loved men too, and there
was no thought of fidelity between them. When Marina
ironically questioned whether Sonyechka spent the rest of
her time alone, Sonyechka replied 'I? I'm a lost soul. I am so
afraid of death that when there is nobody around – there
are such dreadful hours sometimes – I feel like climbing on
the roof to find the cat, just so as not be alone. And not to
die alone . . .'[36]

Marina lost track of Sonyechka in the year she found her.
There was no goodbye. It was from someone else that she
learned of Sonya's departure the day before, and the person

who brought the news was astonished that she had not come to say farewell to Marina. No one knew exactly where she had gone. For Marina, her room grew suddenly cold at the news; the walls and floor faded in colour; everything became dull and grey at once. She felt neither insult nor betrayal in Sonyechka's surprise departure. She understood that Volodya had come because he couldn't leave without saying goodbye. Sonyechka didn't come because she *couldn't* say goodbye.

Many years later, reflecting on what she had lost, Marina said: 'She was my sugar. I needed her like *sugar*. We all know – sugar is not necessary and one can live without it as we all did in the four years of the Revolution, replacing it with treacle or scraped beetroot or saccharin or nothing – drinking plain unsweetened tea. One doesn't die of that. But one doesn't live, either.'[37]

Throughout 1918 and 1919, the conditions in which Tsvetayeva lived with her two children grew daily more difficult. By September 1918, she needed to make forays into the countryside to barter for food. It was a dangerous journey, to and from Usman station in Tambov province, which she wrote about with a certain wild glee. Even when the second train arrived at Usman near midnight she was far from safe. There was only a house with accommodation to let and Marina slept in the clothes she had brought with her, woken by a heavy knock in the middle of the night, the sound of feet, laughter and swearing. By matchlight, it was difficult to make out what was happening, but it turned out to be yet another official 'requisition' squad. Tsvetayeva jotted her impressions of the search as follows:

Cries, tears, the tinkling of gold coins, bare-headed old women, featherbeds ripped open, bayonets . . . they rummage everywhere.

'Doing pretty well with your icons, aren't you! All this for the saints, too! Gods like gold too, I suppose.'

'But we haven't got anything . . . Listen to us. Young man! You'll be a father, too, one day!'

'Shut up, you old crone!'

A candle flame flickers and dances. Huge shadows of Red army soldiers on the walls.[38]

Tsvetayeva was not a shrewd businesswoman, and her bargaining got off to a bad start. The peasants resented everyone who came from Moscow, convinced that no Muscovite could know anything about hard work. Tsvetayeva records how she ended up buying a wooden doll and a necklace of dark amber and giving away three boxes of matches. She was angered by the peasants, though afterwards she came to feel that she had more in common with them than with some of her boorish fellow-travellers.

Aside from such countryside forays for food, Marina decided to improve the family's situation by letting out rooms, and contacted Iks, a decent if humourless Communist, who felt sorry for her. He first suggested she might get a job as a file clerk at the People's Commissariat for Nationalities, which was located in the same building as the Cheka, the secret police. Iks had to reassure her that she would not be involved in working for the Cheka itself (they would have been unlikely to take her anyway). What finally convinced her was the building, the Sologub family mansion, which she believed had been Tolstoy's model for the Rostovs' house in *War and Peace*.

Marina found herself, therefore, on 13 November 1918, in the Information Department of the Commissariat for Nationalities. The burden of looking after Irina fell largely on Alya. Journal jottings of the time give a sharp picture of Marina's monotonous work.

> I am compiling an archive of newspaper cuttings. That is to say, I put down in my own words what Steklov and Kerzhentsev say, reports on prisoners-of-war, the advance of the Red army and so forth. I set down one and then another (I transfer them from the 'journal of newspaper cuttings' on to 'cards'), and then glue these cuttings on to huge sheets of paper. The newspapers are thin and the type is hardly readable, but to write headings in a lilac-coloured pencil and then more glue is totally useless, and it will vanish into dust even before it is burned hereafter.[39]

Marina needed the money urgently, and she hung on to the job, even though she hated it, for five and a half months. She was fair enough to note, when she resigned, that 'under the old regime they would have kicked me out as soon as they took one look at my work'. Soon afterwards, she found herself a job in the Institute of Noblemen, a government department in which she was expected to deal with index cards in a room resembling a coffin, supervised by a woman who behaved like a gaoler, ironically amazed at how slowly Marina worked. She commented acidly: 'Our normal quota is 200 cards a day.' Even the knowledge that her children depended on her for food did not prevent Marina from walking out after a single morning.

This was one of the last of Marina's actions to be characterized by a kind of spoiled child's refusal to accept responsibility. It was not the noble gesture she made of it in *My Jobs*, in which Tsvetayeva explained: 'My feet took me out without my being conscious of it. This is what is called instinct.'[40]

On 14 July 1919, it took more courage and some insolence, when offered a reading at the Palace of the Arts, to choose a group of poems that condemned the three-fold lie of 'freedom, equality and brotherhood.' She was to be paid sixty roubles for the reading, but she refused the money. It was only paper of course, and would have bought little, but the gesture had an arrogance in keeping with her refusal to perform menial work.

In the famine of 1919 the money would have bought only a pound and a half of flour. Marina could not have survived without the help of friends. Some gave her the occasional luncheon voucher; an actress brought some potatoes and some beams ready sawed for fuel; a literary friend brought matches and some bread. However, the squalor and poverty of the family situation was unremitting and would have been so for even the most careful housewife. This Marina was not. In her journal, she noted:

I live with Alya and Irina (Alya is six, Irina two years seven months) in our same flat on the lane of Boris and Gleb, opposite two trees, in the attic room which used to be Seryozha's. We have no flour and no bread. Under my writing desk, there are about twelve pounds of potatoes which is all that is left from the food 'lent' by my neighbours. These are the only provisions we have.[41]

This laconic catalogue of resources is very far removed from the usual voice of Marina's daily record of her life. It reads like a sober note to a future reader after Marina's death, recording the details of her desperation. Marina meanwhile walked all over Moscow looking for bread for sale. Whatever she managed to beg or buy, she usually carried back without help. If Alya came with her, Irina had to be left alone, tied into her chair for safety. Marina's journal makes her stress clear:

I feed Irina, then put her to bed. She sleeps on the blue armchair. There is a bed, but it won't go through the door. I boil up some coffee, drink it, and have a smoke. I write. Alya writes or reads. There is silence for two hours. Then Irina wakes up. We heat up what remains of the mashed goo. With Alya's help, I fish out the potatoes which remain, or rather have become clogged in the bottom of the samovar. Either Alya or myself puts Irina back to bed. Then Alya goes to bed. At 10 pm the day is over.[42]

Marina depended on Alya not only for help in grappling with slop buckets and wood chopping, but also for spiritual assurance. In some ways the relationship recalled the few moments when Marina had been closest to her own mother. Terror and responsibility drew the bond between Marina and her daughter more tightly. They often slept in the same bed for warmth, sometimes fully clothed.

Everyone was hungry, all the time. Irina once tried to

stuff a raw cabbage into her mouth. And she looked sickly. In June 1919 her former nanny, a peasant from Vladimir province, begged Marina to let her take the child back to her village where there were still potatoes and milk. Her kindness staved off the child's hunger for several weeks. Meanwhile Alya fell seriously ill and Marina kept her alive only with a tremendous struggle. When Irina returned it looked as if she could survive only in a state orphanage. The decision was tragically mistaken. Irina – whom Alya described as a little girl with a straight forehead, fair ringlets and grey eyes, always singing 'Maena [Marina], my Maena' – died of hunger in the winter of 1919/20, at the age of two years ten months, in the care of the orphanage that Marina had hoped would save her.

Marina wrote to her sister Anastasia in December 1920:

Forgive me if I keep writing the same things – I'm afraid of letters not getting through.

In February of this year Irina died – of hunger – in an orphanage outside Moscow . . . Irina was almost three. She could hardly speak yet. It used to be distressing to see her. She would spend all the time rocking and singing. Her ear and her voice were astonishing – if you should find any trace of S., write [him] that it was from pneumonia.[43]

SIX

Marina was in pain whenever she remembered Irina, or allowed herself to be chilled by the thought of Seryozha's possible death. She and Alya now lived in the dining room of the flat on Boris and Gleb Street, and to heat that one room they had to burn the furniture from the others. They were not altogether isolated; others battled against the same conditions. When Marina met Boris Pasternak in the street, he was on his way to sell valuable books from his family library to buy bread. They were not close friends, but they felt themselves to be part of the same community of poets, even though their politics were widely different at that time.

The February Revolution had filled Boris with exhilaration, as if 'the lid had been snatched off the whole of Russia'. Although the fine poems of his book *My Sister, Life* make little reference to particular events of the year of revolution, he himself 'saw on earth a summer that seemed to recognize itself – natural, prehistoric, as in a revelation'. On one point, however, Marina and Boris could have agreed: by the spring of 1920 the worst of the famine was over, at least in

Moscow. Marina was allocated a government ration of food, and this led her to encourage her sister to return from the Crimea to Moscow. From Voloshin's letters, she knew how disastrous the situation was there. Corpses were being eaten; and in the last month of her life, before she died from emphysema, Pra ate eagles. Marina wrote:

Asya! . . . Come to Moscow. You have a miserable life. Here things are returning to normal, but it will be a long time before that happens where you are. We have a lot of bread; there are frequent distributions for children; and – since you insist on having a job – I could arrange (my great connections!) a wonderful position for you, complete with large rations and firewood. Apart from that, you would be a member of the Palace of the Arts (formerly Sologub's) and receive three decent meals for almost nothing. Forgive the household themes, but I want to get them over with at the start. You will be all right in Moscow; there are many acquaintances and semi-friends; I have relations; we will manage. *You can be sure of it.*

I hate Moscow, but at the moment I cannot travel, because this is the only place [Seryozha] can find me – if he's alive. I think of him day and night. I love only him and you.

I'm very lonely, even though all Moscow is full of acquaintances of mine. They are not people – believe that literally – or else they are already so worn out that I, with my temperament, feel awkward, and they feel perplexed.

All these years I have always had someone next to me; but still felt utterly desolate in my need for people![44]

It was clear that the old way of life had gone for ever: 'I no longer hold anything dear except for the maintenance of my rib-cage. I am indifferent to books; I sold off all my French ones; whatever I need, I shall write myself!'

In December, Marina had heard from Ilya Ehrenburg that her brother-in-law Boris was dead, but she had refused to believe it. She was too superstitious about Seryozha's survival. A postscript in the same leter to her sister makes that clear.

If I knew [Seryozha] was alive, I would be completely happy. I need nothing apart from you and him.[45]

Marina's letter to her sister suggests that she had little time for the literary life around her, and she complained that her work was rarely allowed to appear in any case, because the poet Bryusov controlled the publication of all literature. Bryusov had been one of the four poets to review *Evening Album*, Tsvetayeva's first book of verse, and he had taken exception to many of the qualities that had so attracted Gumilyov. He would hardly have become so bitter an enemy, however, if the eighteen-year-old girl had not, in return, written an angry letter to him about his attitude to Rostand and, later, directed a mocking poem at him, accusing him of following fashion blindly. In spite of this undisguised antagonism, Marina was allowed to take part in the life of the Palace of the Arts, where three, nearly free, meals a day were available. The restaurant was a place where it was possible to meet and exchange gossip with writers of every political persuasion. There, in 1920, she was allowed to read her poem *Tsar Maiden*, and in the winter of 1921 was invited to take part in a reading by 'women poets' organized by Bryusov. That grouping Marina found an insult; she did, however, agree to take part. As Bryusov introduced them all with arch references to the feminine skill in writing of love and passion, her fury was confirmed. In contrast to the frilly dresses of the other women, Marina chose to dress in a belted leather cassock and grey felt shoes. When her turn came, she mounted the platform and read poems from *Swan's Encampment* praising the White army. This was more than a wilful risk, as Marina knew, and she later wrote of it as 'obvious insanity'. As she put it:

I was guided by two, no, three, four aims: (1) seven poems by a woman without the word 'love' and without the pronoun 'I'; (2) proof that poetry makes no sense to an audience; (3) a dialogue with anyone, a single person, who *understood* (perhaps a student); (4) and the principal one: fulfilling, there in Moscow of 1921, an obligation of honour. And beyond any aims, aimlessly, stronger than aims, a simple and extreme feeling of: *what if I do?*[46]

Among the most important readings she attended were those of Alexander Blok. Marina had always admired him with fervour, and had begun writing a cycle of poems for him in 1916. She felt a reverence for his genius, which, for her, surpassed that of all living poets.

> Your name is a – bird in my hand
> a piece of – ice on the tongue
> one single movement of the lips.
> Your name is: five signs,
> a ball caught in flight, a
> silver bell in the mouth

a stone, cast in a quiet pool
makes the splash of your name, and
the sound is in the clatter of
night hooves, loud as a thunderclap,
or it speaks straight into my forehead,
shrill as the click of a cocked gun.

Your name – how impossible, it
is a kiss in the eyes on
motionless eyelashes, chill and sweet.
Your name is a kiss of snow,
a gulp of icy spring water, blue
as a dove. About your name is: sleep.[47]

She had the opportunity to hear Blok read twice in 1920. Characteristically, she did not risk introducing herself to him. Instead, at the Palace of the Arts reading, she sent Alya to him with an envelope containing some of her poems and a letter, as if she wanted him to meet her poems, rather than herself as a person. Later, she was to regret having missed the opportunity.

By the time Marina and Alya arrived at the Palace of the Arts all the pink velvet seats were taken, and it was only through Antokolsky that chairs were found for them before Blok arrived. Even as they sat down, an excited whisper went around the crowd: Blok was about to appear. He did not share the excitement of the audience. His eyes were lowered; his face was a dull brown and his mouth looked dry. There was a completely dead expression in his eyes and on his lips, and his whole face looked as if it had been stretched over his bones. When the audience clamoured to hear *The Twelve*, Blok refused: this was his controversial poem in which Christ suddenly appears at the head of a group of ruffians and drunks who bear the standard of the Revolution. He could not read it, he said simply. And the audience understood this as a failure of health and energy. The 'tender spectre', the unkillable spirit of Marina's lyrics, had become a sick man whose hold on life was failing. He died in August 1921.

Tsvetayeva came to know Konstantin Balmont well at about the same time as she failed to encounter Blok, the more easily because Balmont's fame was fading and she was sorry for him. Before the Revolution he had been a legendary figure, but in 1920, when the new government organized a jubilee for him at the Palace of the Arts, there was not much applause. Balmont was already yellow in the face and wrinkled, with misty eyes, a bumpy nose and a strange, lost-looking smile. He no longer made jokes, and he spoke with a slight pause between every word. Even his serenity suggested loss: the fire was gone, the tranquillity was grey. All this was enough to make Marina gentle. However, her circumspection arose chiefly from an observation of his closeness to his wife. Elena accompanied him everywhere: a small, thin, vibrant creature with huge violet eyes who saw to his every need. Marina also helped Elena, waiting with her in one shopping queue after another, and even harnessing herself to Alya's sleigh to help Elena carry frozen potatoes and fuel home to the Balmont house. In addition,

Marina was generous: when she received her ration of two ounces of tobacco she poured out half for Balmont, and there were occasions when he and Marina would smoke a single pipe together to economize on tobacco, sharing puffs like Red Indians. The Balmont flat was heated by a small, sooty stove that Elena tended while Balmont wrote his poetry.

When the Balmonts began preparing to go abroad, they were understandably hesitant, and indeed they kept changing their minds altogether. Marina and Alya eventually saw them off twice. On the occasion of their first departure, the Scriabins gave a farewell party when everyone was served potatoes with pepper (a luxury), and real tea in porcelain cups. The next day, however, some trouble arose over the Balmonts' Estonian visa, and their departure was delayed. The final farewell took place in an indescribable mess. There were clouds of tobacco smoke and samovar steam, as the Balmonts left their house rather as gypsies might strike camp.

Marina herself was not ill-treated officially and in the winter of 1921 she made friends with P. S. Kogan, a convinced Bolshevik, and his wife. Kogan believed that no good writer could really be hostile to the Revolution. She was given a ration card, and some of her strangest poetry, including a folk tale of magic and incestuous love, was accepted for publication.

Marina's sister had returned from the Crimea the previous spring with tales of people staying alive by boiling moss.

Gaunt and ragged though she was, Asya was determined to go out and find a job and, ironically, found one at the very museum that their father had founded. Asya's contact with Soviet officialdom was less successful than her sister's. By coincidence, the new regime had installed as director a young man, little enough qualified for the post, who had once been a suitor to both the Tsvetayeva daughters. They had been contemptuous of him then; now the reversal of fortune was complete and he told her briskly that there was no job available. A week later, however, a letter arrived with the offer of a low-paid job as a non-staff employee.

There was still no word from Seryozha. Ilya Ehrenburg looked at Marina's cycle of poems *Swan's Encampment* in the autumn of 1920 and tried to explain how differently her heroes of the White army had been behaving. Evidence of the looting and murder of innocent villagers was, in fact, overwhelming; but she was too obstinate to believe any account of brutality in an army that included her tenderly loved Seryozha. And even she had to acknowledge that the civil war was beginning to resolve itself into a Bolshevik victory.

Even as the fact of peace was assimilated, a new threat began to show itself: the intelligentsia both in Petrograd and in Moscow (always suspect in Russia) suddenly found their political credentials were to be seriously examined by the victors. Among many others, Akhmatova's divorced husband, the poet Gumilyov, was arrested. The uneasy atmosphere of August 1921 was caught by Nina Berberova, as she described how everyone first learned to speak in whispers in the Writers' House and the House of the Arts in Petrograd.

> Everywhere there was silence, waiting and uncertainty. The 24 August arrived. Early in the morning, when I was still in bed, Ida Nappelbaum came over. She came to tell me that on the street corners were posted the announcements: all had been shot . . . sixty-two persons in all . . . That August was not only 'like a yellow smoke' [Akhmatova]; that August was a boundary line.[48]

Akhmatova was a poet whose excellence had excited Marina to write a cycle of poems for her in 1916. Their names were always to be linked as equals, although the two poets had very different personalities. For one thing, Akhmatova was an acknowledged beauty, whose style and pride had already been caught in a line drawing by Modigliani, and many men had fallen in love with her. Yet for Gumilyov she continued to feel the bond of a love that had never been equally requited. He was, moreover, the father of her only son. When she heard of his execution, she was struck with despair. She must also have understood her own danger. In Moscow, rumours began to circulate that she had taken her own life.

The passion that went into Marina's letter to Akhmatova of 31 August, offering her loyalty, was characteristically reckless.

31 August (O. S.) 1921

Dear Anna Andreyevna,
Of late, gloomy rumours have been circulating about you,

becoming more persistent and unequivocal with every hour that passes. I write to you about this, because you will hear in any case. I want you to be correctly informed, at least. I can tell you that, to my knowledge, your only friend among poets (a friend indeed!) turned out to be Mayakovsky, as he wandered among the billboards of the 'Poets' Café' looking like a slaughtered bull.

I have, in the hope of finding out about you, spent these last few days in the Poets' Café. What monsters! What squalid creatures! What curs they are! Everything is here: homunculi, automatons, braying stallions and lipsticked sleeping-car attendants from Yalta . . . [49]

Marina went on to give an account of a contest between poets who wished to be considered as full members of the Writers' Union. She had sat impatiently through this, until at last she had to send up a note to Aksyonov on the platform to beg for true news of Akhmatova's fate. She took his nod to mean that Akhmatova was alive.

Dear Anna Andreyevna,
To understand what yesterday evening was for me, to understand Aksyonov's nod to me, one would have to know how I lived the previous three *unspeakable* days. A horrible dream. I want to wake up, but I cannot. I confronted everybody, beseeching your life. A little longer and I would have actually *said* 'Gentlemen! See to it that Akhmatova be alive!' . . . Alya comforted me: 'Marina! She has a son!'

———————

At the end of yesterday's proceedings, I asked Bobrov's permission to make an official journey – to Akhmatova. Laughter all round.

'Gentlemen! I will give readings – ten evenings in a row for nothing –and I always have a full house!'

––––––––––

These three days (*without you*) Petersburg ceased to exist for me – Petersburg! . . . Yesterday evening was a miracle:

'You became a cloud in the glory of rays.'

I shall, in the near future, give a lecture about you – the first time in my life: I harbour a loathing for lectures, but I cannot yield this honour to another! In any case, all that I have to say is; Hosanna!

I conclude as Alya concludes letters to her father:

Kisses and deepest respect, M. Ts.[50]

Although too aware of Akhmatova's pain to mention that her own ordeal was ending, Marina now had definite news from Ehrenburg that Seryozha was alive. In the spring of 1921, as one of the first Soviet citizens to go abroad, Ehrenburg had discovered that many soldiers from the defeated White army had made their way to Prague and been given places at the university, and that Seryozha was among them.

Marina at once applied for a passport to go abroad. Afterwards, her daughter was to reflect that Marina made two decisions because of Seryozha for which she was to pay bitterly: the first was to follow him into exile; and the second was to follow him back to the Soviet Union before the outbreak of the Second World War.

The terror she felt in the succeeding weeks resulted from an almost overwhelming anxiety that the miraculous possibility of seeing and holding Seryozha again would be denied her by malevolent fortune. There was nothing political in her decision to go abroad, and it is extremely unlikely that she realized the enormity of her decision – or its inexorable results.

On 1 July 1921, at ten o'clock in the evening, Marina received the first letter from Seryozha. For him the news that Marina was still alive had been transfiguring and had sent him wandering about the town, all day long, out of his mind with joy. Their dependence upon each other was deep and equal: Marina needed, above all else, the certainty of being wanted and irreplaceable; and to Seryozha she represented the only secure and protective love he had known since his mother had died. Seryozha wrote:

Our meeting was a great miracle, and our future meeting will be an even greater one. When I think of it – my heart stops beating – frightening – for there could be no greater joy than the one that awaits us. But I am superstitious – so I shall not talk about it . . .

All the years of our separation – every day, every hour – you were with me, in me. But, of course, you must know that already.

It is hard to write about myself. All the years I have spent without you have been like a dream. My life is divided into 'before' and 'after', and 'after' is a terrible dream, I'd like to wake up, but I can't . . .

What can I say about my life? I live from one day to the next. Every day is struggled for, and each one brings our meetings nearer. This last gives me happiness and strength. Otherwise everything around is very bad and hopeless. But I'll tell you all about that when we meet.[51]

Marina's own journal notes for this period are incoherent, and, like Seryozha, she had a superstitious fear of being happy.

Just before her departure, Osip and Nadezhda Mandelstam knocked on her door. Delighted as she was to see Osip again so unexpectedly, Marina could hardly bring herself to offer Nadezhda her hand. Indeed, if Madame Mandelstam reports her correctly in *Hope Abandoned*, she behaved with abominable rudeness, saying to Mandelstam, 'Let's go and see Alya,' and then adding to Nadezhda without so much as a glance: 'You wait here. Alya doesn't like strangers.' Accordingly, the total disorder of Marina's rooms at this time was recorded with wry detachment in Madame Mandelstam's memoir.

Like all former upper-class apartments, it was now given over to dust, dirt and decay, but here there was also an atmosphere of witchcraft into the bargain. The walls were hung with stuffed animals of all kinds, and the place was cluttered with old-fashioned toys which the Tsvetayeva sisters – all three of them in their turn – had no doubt played with as children. There was also a large bed with a bare mattress, and a wooden rocking horse. I thought of all the giant spiders that might be lurking unseen in the darkness, the mice frisking about, the Lord knows what other vermin beside; all this was supplied by my spiteful imagination.[52]

By the time Marina and Alya came to leave, they were living in three rooms: the dining room, the nursery (which may explain the toys and rocking horse) and Marina's own room.

Alya describes their last day in Moscow, packing up,

with great poignancy. So many things had to be left behind. Some of them were deeply prized, not as *things* but because they were so completely imbued with memories. (Marina's sister was deputed to take away as many of them as she could.) There were favourite books, portraits of Seryozha, the music box that had belonged to Marina's mother, the photographs of Marina and Seryozha in their youth, Marina's childhood notebooks.

All the valuables they did take were listed in one of Marina's notebooks, with a few extra notes appended by Alya:

Pencil-case with the portrait of Tuchkov IV
The Chabrov inkwell with the little drummer boy
The plate with the lion
Seryozha's glass-holder
Alya's portrait
Sewing box
Amber necklace
[*In Alya's hand*]
My felt boots
Marina's boots
The red coffee pot
The new blue bowl
Primus, needles for the primus
Velvet lion[53]

The 'plate with the lion' was heavy porcelain with a golden-brown design showing 'a king of the beasts with the face of Max Voloshin'; the silver glass-holder with Seryozha's in-itials had been a wedding present. Marina also chose to take a plush rug that had been her father's last present to her, some hand-made toys and, rather unexpectedly, a Soviet alphabet book with cartoons of Lenin wearing an apron and bow-legged imperialist enemies flying into a ditch. Her listed objects were sacred to her, and, except for one, she was never to be parted from them through all her wanderings until she brought them back to the Soviet Union in 1939. The rough amber necklace with a coarse waxed thread, however, was exchanged for bread by Alya long afterwards during a hungry year near Ryazan. The actor Podvaetsky-Chabrov, whose inkwell is on the list of treasures, was packing to go into exile at the same time as Marina, and he helped her on the final day of departure. Marina liked Chabrov's sharpness, and his ability to see the funny side of the most extreme disasters. However, the great difference in their lifestyles precluded any more than a gay camaraderie, for as she pointed out rather dolefully in a letter to Ehrenburg, 'He is a nobleman, able to live a pampered life, while I? Who am I? Not even bohemian.'[54]

The moment of departure arrived. Marina sat in a cab, with her daughter on her lap and her luggage around her feet, and crossed herself as she went past the familiar white church of Boris and Gleb. She told her daughter to do the same. In that way she chose to say goodbye to Moscow, ceremonially recognizing each church as they passed it.

There were no crowds and not much noise as they arrived for their train. Chabrov gave her a prettily wrapped parcel for the journey, which turned out to be a box of sweets. Alya recorded that Marina snatched the box from her hands, before she had time to do any more than peep at the NEP-style* brunette on the cover, saying: 'How moving! We'll take this to Papa.' Chabrov also passed a message in to them saying that Isadora Duncan was travelling in their carriage. The interesting tit-bit of information turned out to be false, as they discovered when the train set off. They had only Miss Duncan's companion, who was following her mistress out of the Soviet Union and looking after eight weighty trunks of the celebrated dancer's baggage. These evidently contained the used relics of Russia: dried-out tubs, hornless oven prongs and tattered bast baskets – a collection of junk that was to bewilder the many customs officials who boarded the train on the journey.

In Alya's sad record of leave-taking, nothing is more conspicuous than the absence of Marina's literary friends of the period. It was, after all, not yet an offence to leave the country. The last friendly, helpful face Marina was to see in Moscow was that of Chabrov, a courteous aristocrat soon to be in exile himself. And Alya remembered the ring of the three bells that were struck before the train began to move: 'So we left Moscow, unnoticed, as if we had suddenly shrunk to nothing.'

---

* Lenin's New Economic Policy (NEP) allowed some limited freedom to entrepreneurial activities.

SEVEN

Tsvetayeva made no attempt to sleep or eat. For the whole four days' journey to Berlin she smoked incessantly, unable to relax or take an interest in anything. At Riga they had to change trains, and waited for almost a whole day. At any other time, Tsvetayeva would have enjoyed that ancient city with its elegant Gothic buildings and the shop signs (keys, biscuits, bottles, gloves and so forth) that hung over the cobbled streets. Just as it was growing dark, they were at last able to change on to the train for Berlin. Then she let her eyes close, and slept sitting up.

To Alya's astonished delight they found themselves looking out in the morning at the landscape of a Germany that resembled a childhood picture-book.

On 15 May 1922, in bright sunshine, they arrived in Berlin to wait for Seryozha's arrival from Prague. A porter was at their side immediately to carry their belongings to a cab. At once, Berlin (which even after the war remained a city of considerable chic) opened out before them, intoxicating after the poverty of Moscow. The coffee might be poor, but the smell of oranges, chocolate and good tobacco was an overpowering reminder of a lost world. Even if the rate of inflation was already alarming, people still looked well-fed and comfortable. Tsvetayeva made for the Pragerplatz, a small, friendly square around which many Russians housed themselves. Ilya Ehrenburg was staying at a pension there and was expecting them. Moreover, to Tsvetayeva's relief, he was there to welcome them, and immediately put a large, dark, book-filled room at their disposal.

Dozens of Russian restaurants had opened in Berlin, with balalaikas, gypsies, pancakes and shashliks. Russian could be heard on every side. There were three daily newspapers and five weeklies appearing in Russian, and in one year seventeen Russian publishing houses were started. At this period, the line between *émigré* and Soviet literature had not yet been harshly drawn, and writers who had aligned themselves with the new regime still met and talked easily with those who had rejected it. And, most important, books from Berlin circulated in Russia itself and were reviewed in the Soviet press.

There were many who found themselves in exile almost by chance, and who were now earning their living by washing dishes or other menial tasks.

Many writers and publishers lived at the pension in which Tsvetayeva and Alya now found themselves. Close by was the Pragerdiehle, a particularly popular café. Often joining Ehrenburg and Tsvetayeva there was the young publisher A. G. Vishniak, who chose to be known by the name of his publishing imprint: Helikon. Marina soon knew all the regular customers of the café well and, as well as Vishniak, made close friends with Ehrenburg's wife, the artist Liuba Kosintseva, and Liudmila Chirikova (the daughter of the famous writer).

At ten, Alya made notes on her impressions of Helikon, which show how much she had absorbed her mother's way of looking at the world.

When Marina looks into his office, she is exactly like an incarnate soul, which troubles and raises someone to its own level, rather than lowering itself to him. In Marina's friendship there is no kind of rocking asleep. She cannot help *pushing* even a child *out of the cradle*. She thinks all the time she is rocking him asleep – but it's a kind of rocking that leaves you not feeling too well. Marina speaks to Helikon like a Titan. She is as incomprehensible to him as the North Pole would be to an inhabitant of the East, and as strangely tempting. I have seen how he reaches towards Marina as if to the sun, like a crushed little stalk. But the sun is far away, because the whole of Marina's being is reserve and pursed lips while he himself is pliable and soft, like a pea shoot.[55]

Tsvetayeva was not found so formidable by people who needed help, and at this time Andrei Bely was living most unhappily close by. In her adolescence she had heard his name uttered reverently by Ellis throughout their friendship, but had never been allowed to meet him. Later on, his marriage to Asya Turgeneva had made acquaintance possible, though never close. Jealous as she was, because of her own infatuation with Asya, Tsvetayeva still forgave Asya's choice of Bely because they were of the same kind, those who *wrote* poems, rather than inspiring them. Tsvetayeva met him in the Pragerdiehle, at Ehrenburg's table. Bely recognized her suddenly: 'You? You? . . . Here? How happy I am! Have you been here a long time? Have you come for good? Were they following you on the way?'

Tsvetayeva knew how to speak with those whose nerves were stretched beyond endurance. At this time, Bely's grief at the break-up of his marriage to Asya Turgeneva had brought him to the verge of madness, but even though her own future was far from settled, Tsvetayeva gave Bely a sense of refuge. In June 1922 he wrote to her:

My kind, kind, kind, kind Marina Ivanovna . . . during these last particularly difficult, burdensome days you *again* sounded the only true note towards me . . . a tender, tender, remarkable note; of trust. There are miracles after all![56]

Some of the fellowship Bely felt for Tsvetayeva came from the fact that they were both the children of professors. Bely had always declared that he would have preferred to be the son of a coffin-maker. Now he took great joy in stressing their closeness, not only as orphans and poets, but also in the very brand they shared as a result of their fathers' profession. For her own part, Tsvetayeva had never felt her father's position in any way oppressive, but she understood Bely's situation and noted in her memoir of Bely, written after his death in 1934, 'every pseudonym is subconsciously a rejection of being an heir, being a descendant, being a son. A rejection of the father.'

At the time of their meeting Bely had not read Tsvetayeva's book *Separation* (which included her poem 'On a Red Steed', dedicated to Akhmatova), published that year in Berlin, so she gave him a copy. The next day she received a letter of incredulous admiration, and his generous response to Tsvetayeva's work led him to place two of her manuscripts, *Tsar Maiden* and *Versts*, with a publisher – a remarkable gesture from someone who was almost incapable of doing anything on his own behalf.

Tsvetayeva did not often analyse the strangeness of those she loved, and she made no attempt to force Bely into taking control of his own life. She responded to his innocence and weakness in the most practical way possible – by heating up his stove in Zossen, for instance, or sweeping away his rubbish.

During the weeks that she was in Berlin waiting for Seryozha, Bely frequently came over from Zossen on overnight trips to see her. Alya (now nine years old) and his publisher's five-year-old son, who was often in the apartment, found him easy to tease, and sometimes put rubber animals filled with water in his bed. This did not particularly distress Bely, whose problems with insomnia went far deeper than the presence of children's toys in his bed: one of his greatest fears was to wake up under a staring face. Tsvetayeva was one of the few people whose presence in the house gave him peace. As he put it, 'she brings sleep to me. I am going to sleep, sleep, sleep.'[57]

To Bely's brilliantly distorting eye, it seemed that what trees there were cast no shadows, and that the birds did not sing. He disliked even the name of the suburb where he lived: *Zossen*. He found it fleshy, 'like noodles for soup'. However, his deepest grief was over the loss of the woman he loved and the jealousy he felt for the man who had supplanted him. His distress was pitiful, and in her attempt to comfort him Tsvetayeva took less notice of Alya, though she always took the child with them wherever they went. Alya was always very quiet on these occasions, as if recognizing that an encounter between two poets was of great importance. For Tsvetayeva, who had always seen Alya as an extension of herself, the exclusion was unintentional: she simply began to overlook the fact that Alya had needs of her own. As a comic instance of this, Alya recalled that on one long walk with Bely she needed to find a lavatory, but was so afraid of interrupting their conversation that she had at last to resort to relieving herself in the open air.

Nothing could be more characteristic of Tsvetayeva's greatness of spirit than her strength to deal gently with Bely in his state of frenzied desperation. For her, it was a time of continuous suspense. The exact date of Seryozha's arrival was uncertain. In the event, the telegram with the time of his train was delayed, so that after weeks of waiting, Tsvetayeva found herself rushing helplessly towards the station to meet a train that had already arrived. There was no message, and Alya and Tsvetayeva began to wander about in the deserted white square, incredulous and confused, until suddenly she heard Seryozha's voice and they were able to hold one another close, weeping, after all their fears.

In a letter to Maximilian Voloshin in the autumn of 1923

(published in Simon Karlinsky's life of Tsvetayeva), Efron wrote of the way his relationship with his wife had changed over the period of their separation: 'Marina is a creature of passions. To a much greater degree than previously – prior to my departure. To plunge headlong into a self-created hurricane has become a necessity for her, the air of her life.' He added bitterly that he had long felt useless himself for stoking the furnaces of her passions, and referred to a brief and unreciprocated passion Tsvetayeva had felt for Vishniak: 'A few days before my arrival, the furnace had been kindled – but not by me.'

The joy that husband and wife felt on greeting one another after the long years apart was nevertheless intense, even if their relationship had changed in character. As early as Seryozha's first letter to Marina of July 1921, he showed that he was aware of this. 'Just go on living,' he declared then. 'I will make no demands on you. I need nothing from you except that you stay alive.'[58]

That night the Ehrenburgs gave a huge party to celebrate the reunion. There was even champagne. Alya's sharp eyes, observing her father, noted:

Seryozha, who was nearly twenty-nine, still looked like a boy who had just recovered from a severe illness: he was so thin and big-eyed and still seemed lonely – even with Marina sitting next to him. She in contrast seemed to have grown up altogether – once and for all! – right up to the threads of her early greyness, which already glittered sharply in her hair.[59]

Seryozha's first visit to Berlin was a short one. He had to

return to Prague to prepare for the next academic term. He planned to study Byzantine art under Nikodim Kandakov and he was not finding the work easy. Before then, however, there were many decisions to be taken. The first was to move out of the Ehrenburgs' large room into a little hotel in Trautenaustrasse, where the Efron family could afford to rent two tiny rooms and a balcony. The most important decision was not so easy to make: it concerned the move to Czechoslovakia.

There would have been financial problems in staying in Berlin. The small fees Tsvetayeva was earning from Russian publishing houses there could easily dry up, whereas at the university in Prague there were grants to help students, provided by Tomas Masaryk's government. Worse, in the economic crisis hanging over Germany at that time, there was little likelihood of a Russian finding a job. In Czechoslovakia, on the other hand, there was a firm source of money, and the sympathetic government was already giving funds to Russian scientists. Moreover, the country was Slav, and the city of Prague itself, as Seryozha described it, was as beautiful as a fairy tale.

Tsvetayeva had been working very hard. During the two and a half months she had lived in Berlin she had seen very little of the city, but she had written many poems, and an essay on the poetry of Boris Pasternak called 'A Downpour of Light'. By a strange coincidence, it was at this time that Pasternak first picked up Tsvetayeva's volume *Versts* in Moscow and was moved to write to her and explain how much that experience had changed him.

The letter from Pasternak arrived on 27 June 1922, forwarded by Ehrenburg; Pasternak had particularly instructed him to read it, presumably to ensure Ehrenburg's continued protection of Tsvetayeva. It is an extraordinary letter, and initiated the correspondence that was to be one of Tsvetayeva's main emotional supports in the long years of exile.

13.vi.22

Dear Marina Ivanovna,

Just now I began reading your 'I know, I shall die at dawn, on one of them' with trembling in my voice to my brother – and I was struck down, as if by a stranger, by a wave of tears which forced its way to my throat and finally broke through. When I transferred my attempts from this poem to 'I shall tell you about the great deception', I was likewise thrown down by you, and when I transferred them to 'Versts and versts and versts and stale bread', the same thing happened.

You are not a child, my dear, golden, incomparable poet; and I hope you understand what that means in our times, when there is an abundance of poets and poetesses, not only of such as are only known to their union, an abundance not only of imaginists, but an abundance even of unstained talents, like Mayakovsky's and Akhmatova's.

Forgive me, forgive me, forgive me!

How could it happen that treading with you behind the coffin of Tatiana Fedorovna Scriabina* I did not know whom I was walking next to?[60]

It is entirely understandable that Tsvetayeva did not reply at once to such praise – and that she chose an unusual way

---

* Scriabin's wife.

of doing so. In her letter to Pasternak, a note almost like anger sounds in the opening. She clearly wanted Pasternak to sense the mixed feelings she had felt when she read his letter for the first time. And her whole letter is tinged, not with reproach precisely, nor with regret, but more with a recognition of loss that she would endure so often, of which her failure to make more than superficial contact with Pasternak in Moscow had been a significant part. And there is something else too: not pride, not shyness exactly, but the same reluctance that had prevented her from going to visit Pasternak before she left Moscow; the same shyness that had prevented her meeting Blok. Tsvetayeva was always capable of the most female, human anxiety: what if I cannot live up to his expectation of me! Here is her reply:*

Berlin, 29 June 1922

Dear Boris Leonidovich,

I write to you in the sober light of day, having overcome the temptations of night and my first impulses.

I have let your letter cool off, become interred under two days' rubble. So what survives?

Well, from underneath the rubble:

Glancing over it, the first thing I felt was an *argument*. Somebody was arguing, somebody was annoyed, somebody was calling me to account: there was somebody I had not settled with. I felt the

---

*The originals of these and other letters to Pasternak have been lost. Tsvetayeva kept rough drafts of all her letters to him; it is from these I quote.

pangs of hopelessness, of uselessness. That was before I had read even a single word.

I start reading (still not understanding who it is) and the first thing that penetrates through the unfamiliar sweep of the handwriting: *he is rejected* – I still do not realize who. (And my unbearable response: All right, so somebody is dissatisfied, indignant. But good Lord! How am I guilty for the fact that he read my poems?) – and only towards the end of the second page, at the mention of the name of Tatiana Fedorovna Scriabina, like a blow on the head . . . Pasternak!

Now hear further:

Some time in the spring of 1918, you and I sat next to each other at dinner at the Tsetlins. You said, 'I want to write a major novel; one with love in it, and with a heroine. Like Balzac.' And I thought: how fine; how precise; how above conceit! A Poet.

Then I invited you: 'I would be happy if you could . . .' But you did not come because novelty in life is unwelcome.

11 April (Old style) 1922, Tatiana Fedorovna Scriabina's burial. She and I were friends for two years. I was the only woman friend she had all her life. Ours was a stern friendship, devoid of the tenderness of earthly tokens.

And so, I accompanied her large eyes on their way into the earth.

I walked with Kogan, then with somebody else, and suddenly, hand on sleeve like a paw – you. (Later I wrote of this to Ehrenburg.) We talked of [Ehrenburg]. I asked you to write to him. I spoke of his boundless affection for you. You listened perplexedly, even dolefully:

'I completely fail to understand why . . . How difficult . . .' (I felt pity for Ilya Grigorievich and did not include this in my letter.)*

---

* This note must be addressed by Tsvetayeva to herself.

'I read your poem on hunger . . .'

'Don't remind me. It disgraces me, I wanted something completely different. But you know, it sometimes happens like that; milling masses above your head; then you look down, and the paper is still white; the poem has floated past, without touching the table. That poem I wrote at the last moment. People pestering me, telephoning me, but it wouldn't come together . . . You know who liked your book very much? Mayakovsky.'*

This was a *great* joy: the gift of all that is *alien*: conquered space (time?).

I truly brightened, inwardly.

And the coffin. White. Without wreaths. And, already close, the comforting arch of the Novodevichii Monastery; blessed repose.

I reflect on Tatiana Fedorovna. Her last moments in the air of this earth. And, with a jolt; a feeling of *dislocation*. It did not occur to me – since I was engrossed with Tatiana Fedorovna – to watch her through to the end.

And when I look round, you are no longer there. *Disappearance*.

This is my last vision of you. A month later, to the day, I left. I had wanted to call in to please Ehrenburg with an eye-witness account of you, but I felt: a house I don't know, and he probably won't be at home, etc.

Later, I was even ashamed to face Ehrenburg, after such weak ardour for his friendship.

That, dear Boris Leonidovich, is my 'History with you' – also dislocated. I know little of your poetry. I once heard you at a public reading. You kept forgetting everything. I had not seen your book.

Soon my book *Remeslo* comes out. Poems of the last eighteen

* The poet and dramatist Vladimir Mayakovsky (1893–1930).

months. I shall send it to you with pleasure. In the meantime, I am sending you two diminutive booklets which appeared here without me – simply to pay for my passage: *Poems for Blok* and *Parting*.

I shall be in Berlin a long time. I wanted to travel to Prague, but the conditions of life there are hard.

Here I am close to nobody except the Ehrenburgs, Bely and Helikon, my publisher.

Write how things stand with your departure. Are you really coming (in the concrete world – that of visas and forms and milliards)? It is fine living here. Not the town (one is like another), but anonymity, space. One can be completely without people. A little like in the Other World.

I press your hand; I await your book and you.

M. Ts.[61]

My address is: Berlin Wilmersdorf
                 Trautenaustrasse 9
                 'Trautenau-Haus'

Tsvetayeva's letter is not entirely straightforward. She did not plan to stay in Berlin, and she was soon to leave for Prague. When news came through of Pasternak's imminent arrival in Berlin, though it was not known whether or not he intended to move into exile, Tsvetayeva (by then living in Czechoslovakia) could have seized this opportunity to travel to Berlin to see him. She did not go, though she was then aware of the possibility that this could be her last chance to meet him. Her decision may have been swayed by the fact that he was to be accompanied by his wife, whom he had married the previous spring – Yevgenia Vladimirovna Lurye, an artist of great beauty. (Tsvetayeva was never to mention his marriage during their long correspondence.) The fares, too, presented difficulties: Tsvetayeva never felt entitled to deplete the family budget for entirely selfish reasons. Nevertheless, when Pasternak invited her to come to Berlin, she considered it and decided against the journey, for reasons that were both practical and perversely her own. In an incomparable letter, she explained them:

> Mokropsy, 9 March (new style) 1923*

Dear Pasternak,

I shall not come. I have a Soviet passport and no certification of a dying relative in Berlin, and no connections to force it through. A visa would take two weeks, at best. (Immediately after receiving your letter, I made the most precise inquiries.) If you had written sooner, and if I had known that you were to leave so soon . . . A week ago, a cursory mention in a letter from Lyubov Mikhailovna Ehrenburg: Pasternak is preparing to leave for Russia . . . And that was it. Everything slipped by, without any mention of the date.

Dear Pasternak, I have nothing, except my *fervour* for you, and that will not help. I kept waiting for your letter, not daring to act without your permission. And I did not know whether you needed me or not. I simply lost heart. (I write in a cheerful fatal fever.) I know that it is too late.

On receipt of your *Themes and Variations* – no, earlier, from the news of your arrival – I said: 'I shall see him.' With your lilac-coloured book, this came to life, turned visible (blood), and I started on a large book of prose (correspondence!), counting on finishing by the end of April. I worked every day without a break. What is the connection? It is clear. I have no right . . . so to uproot myself. I

* Gregorian Calendar. All subsequent dates are so set out.

(those surrounding me) have a very difficult life. With my departure, all this damned routine falls on them. I began fervently. Now it is too late. A book there will be, but no you. I need you, not the book.

One final word: and this is no wily cunning. You will remember me more if I don't come. *Not* more – that's a lie. No calculation (I shall remember too much if I see you! *Too much* in any case; it could not be more!), and no cowardice (to disappoint, to be disappointed).

Now about Weimar [where Pasternak had suggested that they meet in two years' time]. Pasternak, don't joke. I shall live by this for two years running ... Pasternak, I was just returning along the rough country road ... I was feeling my way. Dirt, potholes, dark lamp posts. Pasternak, with what force did I then think of you; no, not of you; of myself without you, of these street lamps and roads without you. Oh Pasternak, my feet will walk milliards of verses before we meet! (Forgive me for such an explosion of truth; I am writing as if about to die.)

Now the prospect of massive insomnia. Springs and summers – I know myself – every tree that my eyes single out will be you. How can one live with this? It is not that you are there, while I am here; the point is that you will be *there*, that I shall never know whether you exist or not. Yearning for you and fear for you, wild fear; I know myself ...

Do not be afraid. There will be only one letter like this ...

My Pasternak, perhaps I shall, one day, really and truly become a major poet – thanks to you! I do have to speak without bounds to you, to unfold my heart. In conversation this is done through silence. But I have only a pen! ...

Pasternak, how many questions I have to put to you! We have not talked about anything yet. In Weimar we shall have a long conversation.

Pen out of my hand ... Must leave the kingdom of words ... Now I shall lie down and think of you. First with eyes open, then with eyes closed. From the kingdom of words, into the kingdom of dreams.

Pasternak, I shall think only good of you, only the real, the important. As if after a hundred years! I shall admit not a single accidental or self-willed thought. Lord, all the days of my life belong to you! As all my poems.

I shall finish writing this tomorrow evening. It is now past three, and you have long been asleep. All night I have been talking to you in your sleep.

M. Ts.

10 March Morning

A whole page is still in front of me, a whole blessed, white page – for everything! ...

There is one poem of mine that you do not know: *A Peasant.* I have lived on it since you (in autumn) and before you (before February). Reading it through, you may be able to clarify a lot. It is a savage work – it was totally unable to part with me. Another of the requests: send me poems. That is just as much a liberation for me as my own. Describe *ordinary life*, where you live and write, Moscow, the air, yourself in space. This is important to me. I can tire (of happiness!) of thinking into 'nowhere'. There are many streets and street lamps. When a person is dear to me, then his *whole* life is dear to me; the most mundane detail is valuable. To put it into a formula: your daily routine is dearer to me than another's existence!

Yesterday evening (I had not yet unsealed your letter, which I held in my hands), my daughter's shriek: 'Marina! Marina! Come here!' (I, mentally: the sky? Or a dog?) I go out. Alya points with an outstretched hand. Half the sky, Pasternak, looking like a wing; a wing in half the sky; unprecedented. There are no words for the colour! Light, becoming colour. And it rushes, wrapping tight half the sky. And I came straight out with 'The wing of your departure!'

I shall live by such signs and *omens* . . .

If in Moscow I should be very much abused for 'White Guardism', do not be distressed. That is my cross. My *voluntary* cross. With you, I transcend it.

Last words: be alive. That is all I need.

Leave your address.

Marina[62]

Pasternak was very unhappy in Germany, for all his pleasure in seeing his parents again. He was disappointed in Bely. He disliked the Russian expatriates in Berlin. And when he found, on visiting the University of Marburg, that his old professor, Hermann Cohen, had died, he had little hesitation in deciding to return to Russia with his bride. Tsvetayeva went on waiting for a meeting with Pasternak as an imagined possibility for most of her life in exile.

Tsvetayeva had begun writing her folk tale in verse, *A Peasant*, many years earlier. It is not difficult to see why she returned to it now. She felt herself increasingly drained of life by her sick, tired husband and the burden of her child. A folk tale about a young girl who falls in love with a vampire struck a chord. She herself was intrigued by the point in the story when the village maiden Marusya (Marina's own childhood name) discovers that her fiancé is a vampire and does not denounce him, even though her mother, brother and, finally, she herself are to be murdered by him.

Tsvetayeva was increasingly aware of the one-sidedness of her relationship to Seryozha, though it was not for many years that she made her first truly despairing comment upon it: 'Marriage and love destroy. It's an ordeal. So thought Goethe and Tolstoy. As for an early marriage, like mine – it is a catastrophe . . .'

She said:

I read a folk tale 'The Vampire' in Afanasiev's folklore collection and I was puzzled. Why is it that Marusya, who is afraid of the vampire, so persistently refuses to admit what she has seen, knowing that deliverance lies in naming it? Why does she say no instead of yes? Fear? But fear can not only make us bury ourselves in a bed, it can make us jump out of the window. No, not fear. Granted fear, but something else as well. Fear and what? When someone says to me, do this and you will be free, and I don't do it, that means I am not particularly interested in freedom; it means that my non-freedom is more precious to me. And what is the precious non-freedom that exists between individuals? Love. Marusya loved the vampire. That is why she never named him, and so lost, one after another, her mother, her brother, her life. Passion and crime, passion and sacrifice . . .'[63]

Whatever her letter to Pasternak of June 1922 suggests, Tsvetayeva had no intention of staying long in Berlin. Her heart at this time was entirely set on living with Seryozha. She imagined with joy some countryside village, preferably close to Prague, with paraffin lamps and water that had to be brought from a well.

EIGHT

Tsvetayeva found herself in the village of Horni Mokropsy, separated from Prague by the river Berounka. There they took a room in a three-room house, which they shared with seven other people, a dog and a few chickens. Nevertheless Tsvetayeva felt happy, as the Efron family were at last reunited, and though it was cramped living in one room they were surrounded by orchards, pine forests and hills covered with lilac. In comparison with their lives during the civil war, they were all living luxuriously. Tsvetayeva was allotted a small stipend by the Czech authorities, in addition to the grant offered towards Seryozha's studies.

Both Tsvetayeva and Alya got up at about 8 a.m. Tsvetayeva cooked breakfast, and Alya made the beds, cleaned the tables and the window-sills, and swept the floor with the landlord's broom. It was an arduous routine. She had to collect the milk, carry out the slops and bring water from the nearby well. She also washed the dishes, while Tsvetayeva made the lunch and sat down to write. Not until the evening was Alya free to read and draw.

Seryozha stayed four days of each week in the students' hostel in Prague, in the Svobodarna. Otherwise he lived in the village, where Tsvetayeva pampered him with cocoa and extra butter on his bread. His was still very thin and tired. After breakfast he sat on his grey bed, surrounded by books, or walked to and fro trying to learn his notes by heart.

In spite of her new responsibilities, Tsvetayeva continued to write furiously. Indeed, the first entry in her Czech notebook (dated 6 August 1922) was made only a few days after their arrival.

By the end of September the Efron family had to make a second move, to a house closer to the forest, which could be approached only by a muddy path. This limited access meant that, in order to shift their baggage, Seryozha had to strap bags and hold-alls over his shoulders, and even ten-year-old Alya had to help.

Despite the discomfort, and the damp, the three of them laughed a good deal, and Tsvetayeva sustained her correspondence with Pasternak.

Mokropsy, 19 November 1922

My dear Pasternak,

My favourite mode of communication is in the world beyond: a dream, to see in a dream.

My second favourite is correspondence. A letter is, as a form of other-worldly communication, less perfect than a dream, but the rules are the same.

Neither can be ordered. We dream and write not as *we* want, but as *they* want. A letter *has* to be written; a dream *has* to be seen. (My letters *always* want to be written!)

Thus, never, right from the start, gnaw at yourself (not even the most peripheral gnawing!) if you do not reply, and do not speak of any gratitude. Any powerful feeling is an end in itself.

I have just received your letter at 6.30 in the morning. And this is the dream you fell into the middle of. I make you a gift of it: I am walking across some sort of a narrow bridge. Constantinople. Behind me, a little girl in a long dress. I know that she will not fall behind, and that it is she who is guiding. But as she is so small, she cannot keep pace, and I take her by the hand. Through my left hand runs a flood of striped silk: the dress.

Steps. We climb them (I, in my dream: 'A good omen' . . .). Striped planks on piles, and below – black water. The girl has crazed eyes, but will do me no harm. She loves me, although not for that was she sent. I, in my dream: 'I shall tame with timidity!'

And then – your letter . . .

'Words on a dream.' It was summer then, and I had my own balcony in Berlin. Stone, heat, your green book [*My Sister, Life*, 1922] in my lap. (I used to sit on the floor.) I lived by it then for ten days, as if on the high crest of a wave. I surrendered to it and did not choke; I had exactly enough breath for those eight lines which, to my great joy, you liked.

One line still causes my heart to sink.

I do not like meetings in real life. Foreheads knocking together. Two walls. You just cannot penetrate. A meeting should be an arch. Then the meeting is *above*. Foreheads tilted back! . . .

I live in Czechia (near Prague), at Mokropsy, in a village hut. The last house in the village. There is a stream under the hill, and I carry water from it. A third of the day goes on stoking the huge tiled stove. Life, as far as its *everyday routines* are concerned, differs little from that in Moscow. Possibly it's even poorer! But there is a bonus to my poetry; the family, and nature. *For months on end* I see nobody at all. I write and walk all morning. There are wonderful hills here . . .

As for what you write about certain coincidences, correspondence, guesses – that really is not, the Lord knows, foreheads knocking together! When I wrote of you, my forehead was tilted back. It was natural that I should see you.

M. Ts.

Pasternak, I have a request. Give me a Bible for Christmas. A German one, and be sure that it is in Gothic type. Not a big one, but not pocket-size either. And inscribe it. I have already been asking Helikon for one for four months – in vain.

I shall carry it with me all my life![64]

In this same letter Tsvetayeva mentioned that she had fallen out with Ehrenburg. The reasons were partly political: Tsvetayeva remained totally opposed to the Soviet regime, even though she had remained in Russia long enough to see its first attempts to put its precepts into practice; but by 1922 Ehrenburg was prepared to justify most of what he had denounced in poems written just after the October Revolution. However, the main reason was personal anger at his attitude towards her. In Ehrenburg's novel *The Life and Death of Nicolai Kurbov*, Tsvetayeva provided the model for the heroine, who is described as a naïve and misguided counter-revolutionary. On his side, Ehrenburg had always been a little put off by Tsvetayeva's mixture of arrogance and lack of practicality, and many years later would write, in his *First Years of Revolution*, of the distaste aroused in him by her Moscow flat covered in tobacco ash and dust. Perhaps she guessed his reaction. For all his early kindness, she did not express a wish to meet him again when she was planning to return to Berlin the following year.

Tsvetayeva's life was soon far from domestic. She knew it was only in Prague that she would find her own place. As early as 2 November 1922 she wrote to Anna Teskovà, President of the Prague Czech-Russian Society, agreeing to give a poetry reading. She had already become a friend of the critic Mark Slonim, and by November 1923 frequently met Roman Jakobson, Vsevelod Khodasevich (whom she had known since she was sixteen) and Nina Berberova (two other former *habitués* of the Pragerdiehle café in Berlin, who had often sat at the same table with Tsvetayeva). She also met the important Russian prose writer Alexei Remizov, though Remizov did not take to her; and Vladimir Nabokov mentions her briefly, in *Speak, Memory*, as a 'poet of genius' met in Prague in the spring of 1923.

She was thought of as one of the most important poets to go into exile, but she was not altogether at ease with her fellow-*émigrés*. With characteristic sharpness, Berberova analysed her impressions of Tsvetayeva at this time as someone who deliberately assumed the role of a misfit and refused to acknowledge it as a disability. She mistook Tsvetayeva's proud courage for arrogance. When Tsvetayeva wrote (in her poem 'Praise to the Rich') of taking up her position 'among the tramps and outcasts' of the world, it was no romantic game. Poetry was her only means of sustaining her self-respect. What Berberova missed was the genuine envy Tsvetayeva always accorded beautiful women such as Berberova herself. Tsvetayeva did not repudiate fashion out of affectation. Since elegance was beyond her means, she wore second-hand clothes and gave very little thought to their appearance. In any case, she was puritanical in her habits, and her attitude towards dress was part of that puritanism. She went to bed late and got up early. Cigarettes were her only luxury and she preferred them strong and masculine. When she worked, all she needed was a mug of black coffee and a cigarette. She never felt the need to leap up or walk about the room, but sat at her desk as if she were nailed to it. There she muttered and tried out words for their sound, sometimes writing with amazing speed, sometimes writing out many alternative lines, one after another, never crossing out those that were rejected. She always used a simple wooden penholder and a thin school nib, and as she worked she literally dug the point of her pen into the notebooks in which she preferred to work.

Tsvetayeva's genuine dislike of the 'good houses' of the Russians came from her childhood, and her distaste for the pressures of ordinary everyday life was at its most intense when she contemplated the soulless search for amusement of those who had no work to do. Tsvetayeva herself had, as she admits in the poem, been brought up as one of the privileged. Her rejection of the rich people around her was tinged with bitterness, for her pride made their condescension unacceptable. Hence the paradox of her great poem 'Praise to the Rich', written in 1922.

And so, making clear in advance
I know there are miles between us;
and I reckon myself with the tramps, which
is a place of honour in this world:

under the wheels of luxury, at
table with cripples and hunchbacks . . .
From the top of the bell-tower roof,
I proclaim it: I *love* the rich.

For their rotten, unsteady root
for the damage done in their cradle
for the absent-minded way their hands
go in and out of their pockets;

for the way their softest word is
obeyed like a shouted order because
they will not be let into heaven; and
because they don't look in your eyes:

. . .[65]

Tsvetayeva still felt protective towards Seryozha and was still happy, simply to see the family reunited. She backed all his projects, including a literary magazine which she allowed to publish her poetry. Nevertheless, as early as the beginning of 1923, friction had begun to develop between herself and her husband. During the years they had lived apart, he had changed. He was no longer able to furnish Tsvetayeva with that 'monstrous trust and understanding' she needed. She felt he resented her 'living soul', and disliked it as other men disliked strong women.

Much of what she objected to, when she reflected upon Ehrenburg (in a correspondence with the Berlin critic Alexander Bakhrakh which Tsvetayeva initiated on 19 June 1923), grew out of her unhappy recognition of the way she had grown apart from Seryozha.

That's how it is with women. Always with women. Or rather that's how men are always towards women . . . I did not want to be a dear child, I did not want to be a romantic monarchist or a romantic, I just wanted to exist.[66]

For his part, Seryozha wanted a cheerful uncomplicated life with a certain frivolity. The Pragerdiehle café-life in Berlin, which Tsvetayeva despised (even while dominating it), would have suited him better than her stern dedication. Sharply as Tsvetayeva described Seryozha to Bakhrakh, however, she continued to pay tribute to his basic nobility (though unquestionably she regarded it as a form of 'sick goodness'), and it was mainly because he could no longer give her the kind of attention she needed that she began to look for it elsewhere.

Tsvetayeva had begun to write to Bakhrakh, after reading a favourable review of her poetry, with a formal elegance. But by the second letter, Tsvetayeva must have known that she wanted something more from Bakhrakh than a literary correspondence, even though he was unknown to her. For that very reason, she suggested, 'everything was possible. An unknown man is the one from whom you can expect anything.' Mainly, the relationship she initiated showed how much she longed for a relationship she no longer enjoyed with Seryozha.

Bakhrakh wrote back tenderly, touched by the thoughts she had revealed to him, and Tsvetayeva confessed how much she needed such understanding. The correspondence grew in intimacy. Whatever Bakhrakh may have written years later about Tsvetayeva's misunderstandings, the letters suggest otherwise. Tsvetayeva's interest was not at first sexual. She makes this clear in her letter of 14 July 1923:

I want you (you are twenty) to be seventy years old – and at the same time a seven-year-old child – because I don't want to think of *any* age. I can therefore be completely free with you because I am talking to a spirit.[67]

Two days later she spelled that out:

I am too old for love. That's a matter for children, and not because I am thirty. When I was twenty,* I said exactly the same thing to Mandelstam, the poet whom you love best.[68]

Tsvetayeva began by rejecting Bakhrakh's claim to be in love with her, and refusing to allow him so to delude himself. Bakhrakh, however, certainly encouraged Tsvetayeva to respond to his infatuation, and it was at his invitation that she considered a visit to Berlin. In a letter of 25 July, Tsvetayeva asked whether he would be able to get permission for her to settle there, and how much she would have to pay for such permission, even while admitting to her own anxiety about moving around big cities where she always felt blind, stupid and helpless. She was clearly hoping their rela-

* Tsvetayeva was actually twenty-three at the time of her affair with Mandelstam.

Maria
Alexandrovna,
Marina's mother,
with her father
Alexander
Danilovich Mein in
the 1900s.

Ivan Vladimirovich
Tsvetayev, Marina's
father, in 1903.

Sergei and Marina,
December 1911.

Marina in 1914.

Andrey Beliy
(1880–1934).

Alexander Blok,
1921.

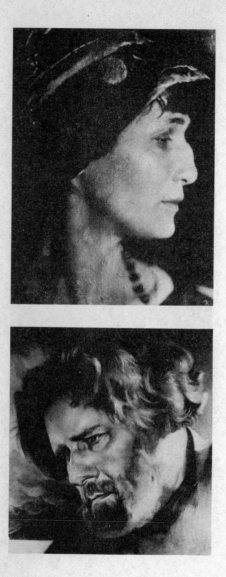

Anna Akhmatova in
the 1920s. (*photo
Nappelbaum*)

Maksimilian
Voloshin at Koktebel
in the 1920s.

Osip Mandelstam,
c.1929. (*photo
Nappelbaum*)

Boris Pasternak
(1890–1960).

Alya Efron, Marina's
daughter, c.1925.

Marina with her son
Georgy Efron at
Clamart, 1933.

Sergei Efron in
Paris, 1937.

Marina Tsvetayeva
in the 1940s in the
Soviet Union.

tionship would develop: 'I am afraid of everything that happens by day and I am not afraid of anything that happens by night.' In the outcome, civil disturbance prevented Tsvetayeva from going to Berlin, but there was no question of her refusing to do so in order to keep Bakhrakh as an ideal and remote figure. In the following month, August 1923, there was a breakdown in postal services between Berlin and Prague. Tsvetayeva feared that the silence meant Bakhrakh had decided to end their correspondence. Ironically foretelling what would most often be said about her, on 19 August she noted:

As if it wasn't enough that I never saw you with my eyes or heard you with my ears – on top of *that*, the unheard voice of the letters has to fall silent! After that I'm told I *imagine* people![69]

That August was in every way a difficult month. Alya was to be sent, at Seryozha's insistence, to Tshebova, a small town in Moravia on the German border, where there was a good Russian boarding school. Parting from her daughter was less difficult for Tsvetayeva than it would once have been because Alya had changed from a precocious child, eager to imitate her mother in every way, into a disappointingly 'ordinary little girl'. Tsvetayeva found the change painful, and said as much in another letter to Bakhrakh:

Alya . . . now plays with dolls and treats me with profound indifference . . . Oh, God must indeed want to make me a major poet, otherwise he would not thus deprive me of everything.[70]

Tsvetayeva had rented a room on the high hill in Smixove

in Prague and she was impatient at losing two weeks helping Alya settle down. She was still suffering from the supposed snub from Bakhrakh, and though she always wanted to be needed, it was not to be simply and functionally necessary as a mother.

While Tsvetayeva was in the forests around her daughter's new school she was at her most superstitious, feeling that Fate was storing up something enormous and terrible for her. Meeting a hunchbacked beggar woman with a bag on her shoulders, she identified the old crone with Fate. Accordingly, she offered all that she had with her, including all of Alya's things, her own shoes, bread and clothes, to be put into the old woman's bag. The woman kissed her hand like a mad creature. Tsvetayeva only partly believed the woman as a supernatural visitation, but she sensed that something momentous was about to happen to her.

It was not Bakhrakh who concluded the love-affair-by-post. It came to an end when Tsvetayeva fell in love with another, altogether real, person present in Prague. When this happened, she knew she must write and admit her new involvement. She did so in September 1923:

Gather all your strength and courage in your hands and listen. Something has ended. The most difficult part is over, now I have said that. I love someone else.[71]

It is very clear from the following letter that Bakhrakh had written back in some indignation, for Tsvetayeva had to amplify her earlier words:

You have not understood my letter. You didn't read it carefully. You didn't take my tenderness, nor my care for you, nor my human pain.[72]

Nothing could make it plainer that it was not Bakhrakh's indifference to Tsvetayeva that led to the conclusion of their relationship. Nor does it seem that either of them intended that that relationship should exist only in their imaginations.

For all the tenderness she continued to feel for Seryozha, Tsvetayeva's own passionate sexuality had found intense physical pleasure only in her love affair with Sophia Parnok. Konstantin Rodzevitch, the man of whom she had written to Bakhrakh, satisfied her desires completely. Thought by many to have been a White officer, he had in fact served with the Red navy for a time but (accurately) judged that things would go better for him in *émigré* circles if he allowed the impression to stand that he had fought on the White side. Although his father, Boris Kazimirovich, had been a general in the Tsarist army, after the Revolution his son served on a ship in the Bolshevik military flotilla on the Dnieper. After being captured by the White army, sentenced to death, then reprieved, Konstantin was persuaded to join the Whites.

Rodzevitch was a man of good manners and great charm, with almost eighteenth-century courtesy; well-dressed, witty in speech, he took a fastidious pride in both his clothes and his person and had a flattering, caressing manner with all women, with whom he enjoyed considerable success.

All this Tsvetayeva found irresistibly attractive. What ensnared her above all else was the way that he treated her as an object of sexual desire, rather than as a celebrated poet. It was his natural mode with all women, but it was new for her. At the very start of their relationship he found it easy to speak 'those great words than which there is nothing simpler' without any self-consciousness, and Tsvetayeva wrote to Bakhrakh that it was like receiving the offer of love for the first time in her life. She was used to casting herself in the maternal, protective role; perhaps she had once found it safer, perhaps even with Mandelstam it was a genuine preference. Now, with Rodzevitch who was known as a ladies' man, she was risking an altogether new kind of relationship. She could not resist what she described in her letter to Bakhrakh of 29 September 1923:

> For the person who loves *me* – the woman in me is a gift; but the person who loves *her* creates a debt I can never repay.[73]

Initially Rodzevitch had been a friend of Seryozha, whom he had met in Prague when they were both students at the university. Of Rodzevitch's relationship with Tsvetayeva, which lasted from September 1923 to 12 December of the same year, Seryozha knew nothing, and if he found that his friendship with her husband made him uneasy, Rodzevitch overcame his guilt. While the love affair lasted, it was a mutual passion, '*un grand amour*', as Rodzevitch liked to call it. Without any literary pretensions himself, Rodzevitch was well aware of Tsvetayeva's eminence. It did not alarm him. He enjoyed dealing with strong women. He had some talent for drawing, and one or two of the sketches he made of Tsvetayeva at this period are remarkably honest; however, a painting on wood made at the same time shows a completely idealized, unlined faced, with her hair untouched with grey. Tsvetayeva was not repelled by the flattery. On the contrary, she found the attention given to her physical person pleasingly unfamiliar.

Tsvetayeva loved Konstantin not only for his good looks and charm, but also for some greatness of soul that no one else imagined in him. Rodzevitch had no such aspiration, and once he was conscious of being in some way admired beyond his merits, he did not enjoy it. He began to feel her power as something 'overwhelming'. In his opinion, love was intended to be a pleasure, and her devouring hunger alarmed him: 'I couldn't bear the tension. I couldn't live up to the hero she thought I was. I couldn't live up to the myth.'[74]

The love affair lasted only a few months, yet they developed a daily ease together, brought out in a lyric from the long cycle of *Poem of the End*, in which she described their favourite breakfast shop.

Even at the height of their love, in November 1923, Tsvetayeva was not so closed in upon herself that she failed to respond to a letter, 'an epistolary howl', from Andrei Bely, begging her to find a place for him in Prague. Tsvetayeva answered at once with the offer of a room next to her own in Smixove, and news that she had spoken to Slonim, who assured her that Bely would receive a Czech stipend of 800 crowns a month. The room she had arranged was never to be occupied, however. Nor was Slonim's offer of a stipend taken up. In November 1923 Bely returned to the Soviet Union. He set out without even waiting for a reply to his letters to Tsvetayeva, as if he had forgotten his impulsive cry for help.

Whatever the reasons for the break in Tsvetayeva's affair with Rodzevitch, it was certainly at his insistence. He claimed to find it unbearable to continue betraying his friend Seryozha. He also claimed political necessity, since he was preparing to engage in active politics and had to disengage himself from Tsvetayeva in order to commit himself decisively to the Left. Whatever his motives, Rodzevitch subsequently set off to marry Moussa Bulgakova, the daughter of a famous theologian, who was well able to provide all the bourgeois comfort Tsvetayeva could not. Tsvetayeva had this in mind in her poem-cycle *Poem of the Mountain*, when she spoke of him returning from the delirium of the love among the pine trees to 'the gentle mercies of domesticity'.[75]

In great misery she turned back to Seryozha, confessing the affair with Rodzevitch and expecting emotional support. Instead he was deeply wounded at the discovery, which came as a great shock. Far from offering to help Tsvetayeva, he drew into himself and his great dark eyes grew even more bitterly unhappy. In the early spring of 1924, Seryozha wrote to his sister in Moscow:

It is bad for me in Prague. I live here as if under a hood. I know very many of the Russians here, but I warm to few of them. And yet in general I get on well with people! I feel terribly warm towards Russia. How soon will it be possible for me to return? Not in the sense of how soon will it be *safe*, but how soon will it be morally possible? I am prepared to wait another three years. I fear that my strength will not last longer.[76]

For the first time in their relationship he considered parting from Marina, and he put the possibility to her even before Rodzevitch had brought her affair with him to a decisive close. Seryozha's suggestion filled Marina with such dismay that she could not sleep and began to lose weight. She was unable to imagine life without Seryozha, and for his part, he felt uneasy about leaving Marina to the mercy of a man whom he saw as a small-time Casanova.

The discovery of Tsvetayeva's deception made Seryozha both mentally and physically ill. Even though they had grown apart, Tsvetayeva had always been the important figure in his life, whose needs he was happy to satisfy, and for whom he had thought himself essential. The extent of her passionate involvement with Rodzevitch made it impossible for him to see himself any longer as a necessary prop to her existence, and that winter he decided to live outside Prague altogether, even though it meant travelling twenty miles a day.

For her part, in January 1924, Tsvetayeva turned to Bakhrakh, not only to explain that her love affair with Rodzevitch was over, but to assess the damage to herself. Not for the first time, she reflected on how much easier she had found it to *love*, than to *be loved*. For her, it had been possible only with children, old men, poets and (however briefly) with Rod-zevitch.

> To be loved is something of which I have not mastered the art ... Dear friend, I am very unhappy. I parted with the ability to love and to be loved at the very height of my love. I didn't part from it, I was torn away from it ... I cannot love myself, because I love; and don't want to, because I love him. I don't want anything apart from him. And he will never be there again ... This is the first such parting in my life, because he wanted everything, he wanted life, he wanted a simple life together. That is something which no one who had loved me before had ever even thought of ... I, who started loving from the moment I opened my eyes, declare I never met anyone like him. With him I was *happy*. I never thought that could happen to me.[77]

In the same letter, Tsvetayeva bitterly commented that she had desperately longed for a son by Rodzevitch. That passionate desire she felt God had denied her, and after their affair ended she was unable to see any baby without feeling the bitterness of having that desire unfulfilled.

She minded Rodzevitch's choice of a successor, whom he married within the year, although she knew that Moussa Bulgakova could offer him a simple, structured home. It hurt Tsvetayeva to think that Rodzevitch had rejected her because he could not live up to her and was unwilling, like Seryozha, to live in her shadow. It augured ill for her future, if the very greatness of her poetry was to bring loneliness and rejection in its train. The foreknowledge of her own isolation led to her bitter identification of poets with Jews.

. . .

> Ghetto of the chosen. Beyond this
>   ditch. No mercy!
> In this most Christian of worlds
>   all poets are Jews.

. . .[78]

Meanwhile Seryozha looked forward to 1925, torn between his desire to continue at the university and the necessity of earning a living. Paris, he saw clearly, would offer more chance of work; at the same time, he was reluctant to leave Prague because it would mean discontinuing his studies. A measure of Seryozha's gloomy spirits at this time was his reflection upon the waste of all his efforts, which he described in a letter to his sister written in that autumn.

Tsvetayeva began her own recovery very much more quickly. She started to work again, transfiguring her misery into two of her greatest poem-cycles: *Poem of the Mountain* and *Poem of the End*. In June 1924 she noted that *Poem of the End* was completed, and although she adds 'but the end in me – how much earlier!' she does not sound spiritually at an end, however much her own misery was exposed in her writing. She must have known she had written her finest poetry so far.

It is in *Poem of the End* that Tsvetayeva gives a profoundly moving description not only of her own pain at Rodzevitch ending their affair, but her sense of the entire relationship. In the first lyric, Rodzevitch appears almost dapper, almost unnaturally courteous.

> A single post, a point of rusting
>   tin in the sky
> marks the fated place we
>   move to, he and I
>
> on time   as death is
>   prompt   strangely
> too smooth the gesture of
>   his hat to me
>
> menace at the edges of his
>   eyes   his mouth tight
> shut   strangely too low is the
>   bow he makes tonight
>
> on time?   that false note in
>   his voice, what
> is it the brain alerts to and the
>   heart drops at?
>
>   . . .[79]

In Lyric 4, she draws the society in which Konstantin and she could move about, almost invisibly, together: a degraded, money-grabbing society, without scruples, like a licentious party.

Throughout Lyric 6, the dialogue between the two lovers has the sound of words etched indelibly on the memory. Konstantin cannot deny his love for Tsvetayeva, but he loves her 'in torment', 'drained and driven to death'.

It is as they walk alongside Prague's beautiful river that the greatest lyric of the sequence (Lyric 8) exposes the whole of Tsvetayeva's misery without any attempt to claim a dignity she cannot feel:

> Last   bridge   I won't
> give up or take out my hand
> this is the last bridge
> the last bridging between
>
> water   and firm land:
> and I am saving these
> coins for death
> for Charon, the price of Lethe
>
> this   shadow money
> from my dark hand I press
> soundlessly into
> the shadowy darkness of his
>
> shadow money it is
> no gleam and tinkle in it
> coins for shadows:
> the dead have enough poppies
>
> This bridge
>
> Lovers for the most
> part are without hope: passion
> also is just
> a bridge, a means of connection

It's warm: to nestle
close at your ribs, to move in
a visionary pause
towards nothing, beside nothing

no   arms no   legs
now, only the bone of my
side is alive where
it presses directly against you

Life in that side
only, ear and echo is it: there
I stick like white to
egg yolk, or an eskimo to his fur

adhesive, pressing
joined to you: Siamese
twins are no nearer.
The woman you call mother

when she forgot
all things in motionless triumph
only to carry you:
she did not hold you closer.

Understand: we have
grown into one as we slept and
 now I can't jump
because I can't let go your hand

and I won't be torn off
as I press close to you: this
bridge is no husband
but a lover: a just slipping past

our support: for the
river is fed with bodies!
I bite in like a tick
you must tear out my roots to be rid of me

like ivy   like a tick
inhuman   godless
to throw me away like a thing,
when there is

no thing I ever prized
in this empty world of things.
Say this is only a dream,
night still and afterwards morning

an express   to Rome?
Granada? I won't know myself
as I push off
the Himalayas of bedclothes

But this dark is deep:
now I warm you with my blood, listen
to this flesh.
It is far truer than poems.

If you are warm, who
will you go to tomorrow for that?
This is delirium,
please say this bridge cannot

end
        as it ends*[80]

*Another verse follows, under a dividing rule. See Feinstein, *Selected Poems of Marina Tsvetayeva* (Hutchinson, 1986), p. 62.

As Tsvetayeva tried to recover from the pain of her rejection, she received letters from Pasternak which confirmed her own sense of development as a poet. And it was a saving joy to receive a letter from him on 14 June 1924: 'What remarkable poems you write . . . How painful that at the moment you are greater than I am . . . You are a disgracefully great poet.'[81] And letters were not to be her only hope of happiness. At about the same time that she received Pasternak's glowing praise, she began to take up less characteristic pursuits – knitting, and other handicrafts – which she followed with enthusiasm because she was pregnant again and convinced the child she was carrying was the son for whom she had always longed. Rumours abound that the child was not Seryozha's – Tsvetayeva certainly carried it with as much joy as if it were the child of Konstantin that she had so much longed for – but the child was born thirteen-and-a-half months after the affair ended and it seems unlikely that her former lover would have risked renewing their relationship.

Tsvetayeva gave up her room in Prague and let herself be isolated from her city friends. All that mattered was her baby. When, in the summer holidays of 1924, Alya arrived in Prague with the beginnings of a tubercular lesion on her lung, Tsvetayeva's first reaction was to fear it might infect the child in her womb. Alya was hurt both by that response and by overhearing Tsvetayeva declare that secondary education was of no use to girls. At eleven, Alya was poignantly beautiful, with wise eyes and a face framed by thick hair. All her early years had been possessed by her mother. They

had faced every hardship in their lives (in the poet Konstantin Balmont's words) 'like two sisters', giving one another love and courage. Now she knew herself rejected
without being freed. From this time onwards Alya's life became more and more subservient to the needs of her mother
(and soon to the needs of her young brother).

Although Tsvetayeva's poetry had begun to find wide
acceptance both in *émigré* magazines and in Moscow itself,
she spent most of 1924 withdrawn from the literary world.
Her poverty as much as her pregnancy embarrassed her.
When Anna Teskovà invited Tsvetayeva to give a reading
in Prague, the latter wrote, on 5 December 1924, 'I don't
know whether I'll manage it on the 14th – train trips are
difficult for me, and I don't have a suitable dress.' However,
she missed the liveliness of Prague, and invited Anna to visit
her country home:

> We'll go for a walk – the surroundings here are marvellous: if
> there is rain or snow we'll sit inside and talk. I'll read poems to
> you. By the way, you will meet my husband and daughter.[82]

Tsvetayeva gave birth to a son at home on 1 February
1925, a Sunday, at midday. It was a simple enough birth,
though not a short one. Tsvetayeva wrote to Anna Teskovà
that 'They said I comported myself well – in any case, without a single scream.' The quiet satisfaction of this assertion
was not proud. She was glad to pay the necessary price of
pain, and recollected the words of a friend who had helped
with the delivery: 'It was *meant* to be painful.'[83]

Her pride lay in the fact that the child was a son. Her original intention to christen him Boris, after Pasternak, brought thunderous objections from Seryozha. Perversely, Tsvetayeva did not persist with her preference when Seryozha finally sighed and gave in. Instead, the child was named Georgy, after the patron saint of Moscow, whose reputation as the protector both of wolves and cattle particularly appealed to her.

Seryozha did not find that the birth of a son relieved his own misery, and he showed little interest in the baby. He felt even more insecure and ill, and determined to live in Paris. Tsvetayeva declared herself to be so happy, as she was so absorbed in her son, that she could hardly bother to take care of her health. At a time when all upper-class women were encouraged to spend weeks lying in to recover from childbirth, she was soon sitting up in bed, and coping well enough; though she had no maid, and even the woman who brought in the charcoal was only a temporary help. The whole organization of the house depended upon Alya.

The financial circumstances of the Efron household had not improved. Tsvetayeva had to write to Anna Teskovà to beg her to send a simple washable dress:

All winter I have been living in the same woollen one, which is falling apart at the seams. I don't need a good one – it is not for a public appearance – just something simple . . . Even a snake must sometimes change its skin. If it is too big, never mind – it can be altered at home.[84]

This letter was written (like so much of Tsvetayeva's poetry at this time) at 3.30 in the morning, when everyone else was asleep and Tsvetayeva had her only chance of time to herself.

When, after the birth of her son, Anna Teskovà at last decided to visit her, Tsvetayeva was so glad to see her, and so delighted to find someone she could talk to about literature, that she forgot to provide either food or tea for her guest. Her absorption in her son is the key to such uncharacteristic lack of hospitality, just as it was in some measure to shape the rest of her life. No wonder Seryozha, already painfully aware of being moved closer to the edge of Tsvetayeva's life than he could bear, found his mood darken as he perceived as much. Tuberculosis, which often recurred when his spirits began to fail, took hold of him once again. By July 1925 he had lost so much weight that he was all bone and huge mournful eyes, and for all his eagerness to live in Paris, he had to enter the Zemgorska sanatorium.

Tsvetayeva began to arrange to leave Czechoslovakia and her friends, to move to yet another country for the third time in three years. As Seryozha was too ill to travel with them, it was impossible for her and Alya to take all their belongings on the journey, and she arranged to store a large basketful with Anna Teskovà. Tsvetayeva was, in any case, unconvinced of the wisdom of the move, and liked the idea of leaving things in Prague for a possible return.

Mark Slonim arranged their passports and helped Tsvetayeva to raise enough money to buy tickets for herself, Alya and Georgy, now affectionately called Moor, a pet name that is variously spelled but always has the soft, purring sound of a pet animal. The train journey filled Tsvetayeva with terror. Without money for even the barest necessities, she could not imagine how she was to deal with her son's food. 'He eats four times in twenty-four hours and everything needs to be warmed for him. How is this to be done? One cannot light a spirit lamp,' she wrote to Anna Teskovà. Nevertheless, she arranged to leave some time after 20 October 1925.

She did not regret leaving Vshenory. The last year and a half had been a period of great isolation, as she described in a letter of 19 July 1925 to Boris Pasternak. Far less lofty in style than those that preceded it, this letter told him candidly about her loneliness and her sense of spiritual poverty. Even so, she continued to work furiously on her poem *The Pied Piper*, which she was not to finish until she reached Paris.

> Vshenory, near Prague
> 19 July 1925

Dear Boris,

The first really human letter from you (the rest are Geistbriefe), and I am flattered, inspired, raised on high. You have just deemed me worthy of your rough draft.

And here is my rough draft, in brief: for eight years (1917–1925) I have been *consumed* by the daily round. I am that goat, whose throat they are constantly slitting and never quite slitting enough. I myself am that brew that bubbles ceaselessly (eight years) on my primus. My life is a rough draft, by comparison with which – oh, you should look! *my* rough drafts are the whitest of white sheets. I despise myself for the fact that at the first call of everyday necessities (1001 calls a day) (N.B.! life's everyday necessities – one's debt to other people), I am torn away from my notebook, and NEVER go back to it. I have a Protestant's sense of duty, compared with which my Catholic – no, my Khlyst [Flagellant] love is a thing of nought.

Do not think of me as living abroad. I live in the country, with the geese and the pump-houses. And do not think: the country: an idyll. No, it means one's own two hands, and not a single gesture for oneself. I do not see the trees. A tree waits for love (attention), and rain is important to me in so far as the washing does or does not dry. Day: I cook, wash, carry water, look after Georgy (he is five and a half months; a *miracle*), study French with Alya; have another look at Katerina Ivanovna in *Crime and Punishment* – that is me. I am furiously embittered. I have been bubbling in the cauldron all day. I have been writing my poem *The Pied Piper* for over three months. I have no time to *think*: my pen thinks. Five minutes in the morning (time to sit down a little), ten minutes in the afternoon; the night is mine, but at night I can do nothing, I am unable to; a different kind of attention; life unlike itself but beside itself and nobody to listen to, not even the noises of the night, since the landlords lock the exit door at eight in the evening, and I have no key (all my doors are entrances; a yearning for an exit. Understand?) . . .

I have no friends. Here they don't like poetry; and what am I apart from – not poetry, but apart from that, *from which* it is made? an inhospitable hostess, a young woman in old dresses . . .[85]

However, the thought of leaving Prague made Tsvetayeva anxious. The city itself enchanted her. She loved the legend of the Golem, that seventeenth-century monster of stone created by Rabbi Löwe to defend the Jews of Prague against their enemies,* and she particularly admired the statue of the knight of Karlov's Bridge, which was supposed to represent a boy guarding the river. To Tsvetayeva, he was a symbol of fidelity – above all, fidelity to himself. She wrote to Anna Teskovà:

> I would passionately like to have a picture of him. Where can I get one? There isn't one anywhere. I want an engraving to remember him. Tell me everything you know about him.[86]

As the day of the family move approached, she tried to comfort herself with the hope that she would find new friends. Certainly she had few of them in the village of Vshenory.

To live with the prospect of a departure that might or might not happen was to put oneself in a state of suspense, and Tsvetayeva found this particularly intolerable. There were several hitches in their plans; another kind of panic. Money Tsvetayeva had been expecting from friends in Paris did not arrive; incoming tenants were expected; Seryozha was still in the sanatorium. Eventually, Alya was dispatched to Teskovà's house and returned with enough money to make the journey possible. Once the loan had been arranged Tsvetayeva set off for Paris with her two children, and so left behind the city in which she had lived so intensely, and which she had come to love more than any other.

---

* It had to be destroyed, partly because it became disobedient, and partly because the feeling grew that its creation was blasphemous. The shattered pieces remain in an upper room of the Alte Neue Synagogue.

NINE

Tsvetayeva arrived in Paris on 31 October 1925 with her nine-month-old son Moor and her twelve-year-old daughter Alya, to stay with Moor's godmother Madame Kolbasina-Chernova. (She had once been Tsvetayeva's friend and neighbour in Prague.) The Chernovas had three rooms in Clamart, a working-class neighbourhood, and the whole family lived in great poverty. Madame Chernova was fond of Tsvetayeva; her daughters knew and admired her poetry; and all of them did their best to let their guests share their meagre life equally. It was an act of considerable generosity to give up one of their three rooms. Although Tsvetayeva knew this, she nevertheless found the lack of space and the lack of privacy tormenting. The room she occupied was often invaded by other people who expected her to take part in the conversation. She explained as much in a letter of 30 December to Anna Teskovà:

There are four of us [Seryozha having arrived by then] crammed into one room. I cannot write at all. I think bitterly that even the most mediocre journalist has a writing desk and two hours of quiet. I don't – not a minute: I am constantly surrounded by people in the middle of conversations which divert me from my notebook. I think almost with joy of my job in Soviet Moscow – on that job I wrote three of my plays: *An Adventure, Fortuna* and *Phoenix* – 2000 lines of poetry.[87]

Tsvetayeva rarely complained about people who helped her in the awkward chores of daily living. Above all, she had learned to love and trust 'those who knit your jumpers and look after your children'. In Paris Tsvetayeva feared that she would not find the same protection, and she began to write of Chernova as if she were a landlady. Yet Tsvetayeva did, at least, have a real desk, given to her by Olga (one of the Chernov daughters), and despite all the domestic pressures she found the opportunity to use it. It was with the Chernovs that she finished *The Pied Piper* – writing and rewriting it, even as she cooked Moor his porridge, and dressed and undressed and bathed him as she had in Vshenory. The 100-page epic transforms the familiar story of the cheating burghers of Hamelin exuberantly with new frenetic rhythms, touching the death of the children at the end with magical lyricism.

. . .

> To live means – ageing,
> turning grey relentlessly.
> To live is – for those you hate!
> Life has no eternal things.

In my kingdom: no butchers, no jails.
   Only ice there! Only blue there!
Under the roof of shivering waters
   pearls the size of walnuts

girls wear and boys hunt.
There's – a bath – for everyone.
Pearls are a wondrous illness.
Fall asleep then. Sleep. And vanish.

Dry twigs are grey. Do you want
scarlet? – Try my coral branch!

. . .[88]

On 4 December, Tsvetayeva again wrote to Teskovà, to beg
a dark dress that would enable her to go out in more interesting company. She was ashamed of her shabbiness in Paris,
as she had not been in Prague. She particularly asked Teskovà not to mention her request to Seryozha (at that time in
Czechoslovakia); all her letters to him were reassuring about
life in Paris. In the event, Seryozha, who arrived in Paris in
late December 1925, found that within about six weeks his
wife had become a celebrity. A poetry reading in February
1926 was widely advertised in all the Russian *émigré* papers,
as far afield as the Berlin daily newspaper *Rul*. Her reception
at the packed hall was tumultuous, and confirmed her position as one of the most important poets of the emigration. And Irina Kotting, a poet who attended that reading,
wrote a poem the day after in which she described herself

wandering aimlessly in the rain, barely escaping being hit by cars, because she had been so overwhelmed by Tsvetayeva's great voice. *Rul* also described the reading as a personal triumph. It established Tsvetayeva as a literary celebrity in the Russian community in Paris.

It was only with difficulty that Seryozha, still much in need of comfort and affection, could take pleasure in her success. The Efron family certainly needed money more than fame. Their practical affairs remained precarious. The threatened reduction by half of the stipend Tsvetayeva received from the Czech authorities would have made her altogether dependent upon the charity of her friends. Over the next year the family moved from their initial perch to a series of flats in the south-western suburbs of Paris. There was no possibility of affording a place in the centre of Paris, even if Tsvetayeva had not felt uneasy there: 'In a city square I am the most pitiable creature, like a sheep that has found itself in the middle of New York.'

Her correspondence with Pasternak took on a new intensity. The ecstatic note Tsvetayeva sounds in all her letters to him might well have alarmed an alien spirit. From the letters Pasternak wrote to her in return, it is clear that his infatuation was by now equal to her own and had begun to affect his relations with his wife, Zhenya. On 20 April 1926 he wrote begging Tsvetayeva to decide the course of their relationship within a year.

Look about you, and in what you see and hear discover your answer; only let it not be guided by your desire to see me, for you must desire this knowledge knowing how much I love you. Send me your answer as soon as possible. If you don't stop me, I will come now.[89]

It was Tsvetayeva who backed away from such involvement, as she mentioned in a letter to Anna Teskovà many years later. Pasternak was to be grateful.

In April 1927 the Efron family settled in Meudon, where a number of other Russian exiles, then as now, clustered together. Their new address – 2 rue Jeanne d'Arc – appealed to Tsvetayeva. At that time Meudon was an attractive enough suburb, with pleasant hills and parkland in and around it. The Efron flat was only a fifteen-minute train ride from Paris, and there was the luxury of a garden for Moor, although the Efrons had to share the house with another family.

In Meudon she found congenial neighbours who were to remain loyal to her for the rest of her life – notably Elena Izvolskaya, the daughter of a Russian statesman, once ambassador to France. Izvolskaya's impressions of Tsvetayeva at that time are remarkably sharp: she describes her as

neither elegant nor pretty: thin, pale, almost emaciated . . . altogether not beautiful, but *icon-like*. She worked and wrote and gathered firewood and fed scraps to her family. She washed, laundered, sewed with her once slender fingers, now coarsened by work. I well remember those fingers, yellowed from smoking; they held a tea pot, a cooking pot, a frying pan, a kettle, an iron, they threaded a needle and started a fire. These very same fingers wielded a pen or a pencil over paper on the kitchen table from which everything had been hastily removed.[90]

By now Seryozha was becoming more and more involved with a political movement in which Tsvetayeva took no interest. The Eurasian movement had been started by Peter Suvchinsky, the musicologist, who with his wife Vera was a near neighbour, and there were a number of supporters living close by, including Elena Izvolskaya. The essential ideal behind the movement was that the Soviet Union belonged both to Europe and to Asia. Among the *émigré* community, supporters were thought of as having Bolshevik sympathies, even though their chief, perhaps grandiose, hope was of reforming (if not overthrowing) the Soviet regime. The critic D. S. Mirsky (Prince Dmitry Svyatopolk-Mirsky, later a Communist) was at this time a member of the group and a contributing editor of its magazine *Mileposts*. Tsvetayeva – who had been hurt by not being included in his anthology of Russian lyrics, and had been once described by him as a 'slovenly Muscovite' – found him now an unexpected ally.

Vera Suvchinsky claims to have effected this dramatic change in Mirsky's opinions. She herself much admired Tsvetayeva's poetry, though she was less patient with her as a person. They had first met in Clamart, in late 1925, when Moor was barely nine months old. Then, Tsvetayeva's refusal to wear her glasses had struck Vera as an absurd sign of her inability to come to terms with the outside world, but she did admire the poet's walk – 'like a she-goat'. This is no compliment in English, but the Russian *kozochka* is. Marina's walk was light-footed, angular and determined.

Following her triumphant poetry reading in February 1926, Mirsky invited Tsvetayeva to accompany him on a visit to London. In the event he was not able to arrange a reading for her there, but Tsvetayeva delighted in her first free weeks in the eight years since the Revolution. She loved London: the river, trees, and children, the dogs, the cats and 'the wonderful fireplaces and the wonderful British Museum'.

According to Vera Suvchinsky, Tsvetayeva spent one night with Mirsky in London. He reported to Vera Suvchinsky that she had appeared, rather to his surprise, in his bed, and that he had been struck by her boyish beauty when undressed. It led to no longer relationship. When she returned to Paris Tsvetayeva found that generous friends had made another break possible, and she and the children spent that summer with Vera Suvchinsky near the seaside, at St Gilles in the Vendée, while Seryozha remained in Paris.

Tsvetayeva's looks improved as soon as she was able to shed the ugly clothes her poverty imposed on her. She tanned easily, as she had in the Crimea so many years before, and though she was still not a lover of sea bathing, she loved to lie in the sun. She also took great pleasure in the increasing health and strength of her son Georgy, now about eighteen months old, and delighted in everything he did. Vera found her attitude towards Georgy infuriating.

She saw how Alya was neglected while Tsvetayeva gave all her love to her young brother. Alya was uncomplaining and showed no desire to compete for her mother's attention.

Tsvetayeva's time at St Gilles was, however, far from completely idyllic. Sometimes it was so cold and windy that everyone had to wear winter coats. Then, although she acknowledged the grandeur of the ocean shore and the sea itself, she felt no fondness for it:

What can I do with the sea? Look at it. That's not enough for me. Swim? I don't like the horizontal position . . . I love the vertical: walking, a mountain, I love the sense of power that results. Before the ocean, I am a spectator: as if I were sitting in a box at the theatre . . . Besides that, the sea either intimidates or makes me grow soft. The sea resembles love too much. I don't like love (that is always a question of sitting and waiting for what love will do with me). I love friendship: a mountain.[91]

Tsvetayeva's letters to Anna Tesková through the summer of 1926 came from St Gilles, where, in spite of the proximity of the beach and sea, she still longed for Prague. She knew herself to be a guest in St Gilles, and Tsvetayeva hated being a guest because of the expenditure of courtesy it entailed. When she looked at a postcard from Prague, she saw in the very trees an invitation to return. At the same time she needed to put the emotions of *Poem of the End* and *Poem of the Mountain* behind her. Perhaps it was healthier, now that Rodzevitch had married, to imagine that the city of Prague no longer existed.

*

Fortunately Pasternak's admiration for Tsvetayeva continued unabated, increased by her integrity in refusing to praise his long poem *Lieutenant Schmidt*. In a letter to Maxim Gorky in 1927, Pasternak tried to enlist his powerful support for the 'huge talent of Marina Tsvetayeva and her unhappy, unbearably twisted fate', and offered to do or write anything that would help her to get back to the Soviet Union. Gorky's refusal to help caused an angry breach between Pasternak and the playwright/novelist, even though Gorky's intentions were far from villainous. He and his wife had known both Marina and her sister as children, and Gorky was still on friendly terms with Anastasia. He was less impressed by Tsvetayeva's work, as indeed was Mayakovsky. Vladimir Mayakovsky was a poet for whom Tsvetayeva had always felt and expressed unstinting admiration, an admiration which, of course, increased her unpopularity in *émigré* circles, where no Soviet poet was acceptable. To read, in a reprint of an article, what Mayakovsky had advised Soviet booksellers was all the more painful:

. . . The bookseller must bend the reader a little more. A Komsomolka [female member of Soviet organization for young people] comes in with the almost definite intention of buying, say, Tsvetayeva. To this Komsomolka one should say, blowing the dust off the old book jacket: Comrade, if you are interested in gipsy lyricism, might I be so bold as to suggest Selvinsky? The same theme but what treatment of it! So manly! . . . Try reading this book of . . .[92]

Hurt though she was, Tsvetayeva bore no grudge, and did not modify her own critical opinion of Mayakovsky's worth.

Tsvetayeva once declared that she had encountered only two people who were her equals in strength: Rilke and Pasternak. Her contact with Rilke, however, was to be entirely a matter of correspondence (although, in her childhood, Marina had once met Rilke's mistress in a fairy-tale castle). It is an imaginary meeting that she writes of in her essay 'Your Death', and their correspondence began only six months before Rilke died. Nevertheless, it was heartfelt and reciprocal. The initial contact between the two poets came in 1925 through Pasternak. Rilke had sent his old friend Leonid Pasternak a letter for his son and had already read some of Tsvetayeva's poetry. On 9 June 1926 Rilke sent Tsvetayeva a long, beautiful elegy that he dedicated to her. In response, Tsvetayeva emphasized that her ardour was 'a kiss without lips', and declared her sense of him as 'poetry incarnate'. A few weeks later he sent her a copy of *Vergers*, a volume of poems he had written in French, which was inscribed to her.

Of all those with whom Tsvetayeva had intense relationships through correspondence, Rilke most unambiguously confirmed her spiritual conviction that poetry offered immortality, not in the banal sense of finding admiration in posterity, but through the holy strength of the act itself. Yet even he, as she wrote to Pasternak, failed her to some degree. She found he lacked ordinary humanity towards the grown-up married daughter of his Saxony first marriage; he had no interest in his grandchildren; and (unfairly) she suspected his interest even in her poetry when she discovered the difficulties he now had with the Russian language. But what really hurt Tsvetayeva was what she felt as Rilke's coldness. He didn't need her letters. Her pride, as she confessed to Pasternak, was wounded.

I am not a lesser one than he (in the future), but I am younger than he. By many lives. The depth of a stoop is the measure of height. He bowed deeply to me – perhaps deeper than . . . it's not important. And what did I feel? His *height*. I knew it before, but now I know it first-hand. I wrote to him: 'I shall not belittle myself; that would not raise you any higher (nor make me lower!); it will only make you *more alone*, on the island where we were all born – all like us . . .' O Boris, Boris, heal, lick clean the wound. Say why. Prove that everything is so . . . Don't lick it clean; *burn it out!* 'I tasted little honey' – remember? What's honey?

I love you. The fair, the donkey-carts, Rilke – all this goes into you, into your vast river (not a sea!). I so miss you. Just as if I saw you only yesterday.

M. Ts.[93]

Tsvetayeva's own misjudgement of the difficult, almost reclusive, nature of Rilke was profound. Fired by her excitement at being in close touch with him, she began to declare a passion he found unwelcome, and overstepped a significant boundary in her letter of 2 August 1926.

Rainer, I want to come to you . . . Don't be angry, after all it's *me*, but I want to sleep with you. Simply to fall asleep and to sleep . . . And nothing further. No, there is something; to bury my head in your left shoulder, my arm on your right one and nothing else. No, something else: to know in the deepest sleep that you are there. And also to hear the sound of your heart. And to kiss your heart.[94]

Even if at this time Rilke had not been already mortally ill with leukaemia, he would have taken fright at her tone, which was not only physically demanding but alarmingly possessive. He wrote back without reproach, but she sensed the change in his feelings, and even wrote him a sad card inquiring 'whether he still loved her?'

When Rilke died, Tsvetayeva broke into a passion of grief. Later she was to write a great poem, 'New Year's Greetings', in Rilke's honour. As she wrote on New Year's Day 1927:

Boris, he died on the 30th December, not the 31st. Yet another of life's blunders. The ultimate trivial vindictiveness of life – against the poet.

Boris, we shall never travel to Rilke. That town is no more.[95]

After describing a recent dream of an ocean liner, which she was sure meant that Pasternak would come to visit her, and remembering London with a certain nostalgia, she returned to consider what was impossible for her in relation to Rilke.

Do you see, Boris; the three of us together in real life – nothing would have come of it anyway.[96]

That her letter to Pasternak concluded with a wish to see Rilke in her dreams is a measure of the dullness that now filled her daily existence. Seryozha was exhausted and his health was deteriorating. (He may well have developed some new debility, since he now took arsenic every day as part of his treatment.) Moreover, the finances of the family were extremely shaky, in spite of money given to Tsvetayeva by Salomea Halpern and others. As Tsvetayeva put it:

We are devoured by coal, gas, electricity, the milkman, the baker. For several months, we have been eating only horsemeat and then the cheapest cuts of it . . . Everything that is three francs fifty a pound – that is, the heart, the liver and the kidneys of course – rather than horsemeat at seven or eight francs a pound.[97]

Tsvetayeva hid the fact from Seryozha that the family was eating horsemeat, but to her surprise, when he did find out, he enjoyed the idea of eating horses' hearts, seeing in it a link to Genghis Khan and his Eurasian inheritance.

Had Tsvetayeva lived by herself, the 1000-franc-a-month contributions of Salomea Halpern and other friends would have made such hardship unnecessary. However, she had two children to support and, moreover, had to raise tuition fees for Seryozha to train as a cameraman, though, as it turned out, the only money he ever earned from the film industry was by working as a film extra.

In the summer of 1927, Tsvetayeva's sister Anastasia, who had been staying with Gorky in Sorrento, came to visit Marina in Paris. Anastasia found that as Alya had grown she had begun to resemble her father, and that her eyes were now also too huge for her face. Two-year-old Moor, on the other hand, looked like neither parent. He had a large frame – 'a little giant' Anastasia called him – and they had to buy him clothes meant for six-year-olds. Anastasia noticed at once that Marina showed a deeper love for her son than for her daughter.

Little as she could afford the extravagance, Marina had bought a good cut of veal to celebrate her sister's arrival and had roasted it in her honour. Unfortunately Anastasia had become a vegetarian, and so, although the Efron family enjoyed the rare dish themselves, they were unable to share it with their guest.

At first there was a natural constraint between the sisters, but by the evening Marina was lying on the couch that served as her bed, chain-smoking and talking as eagerly as in the old days. And yet, as she explained how her days were used up by trips to the market, dragging herself home again with the shopping, it was clear that Marina no longer coped cheerfully with her everyday worries. In the chaos of the flat in Boris and Gleb Street, she had looked stronger than she did now in these small new rooms, dressed in an apron, by a gas cooker, in a foreign city. Anastasia in turn told of her friendship with Gorky, and Tsvetayeva was so grateful to hear of it that she wanted to write and thank him.

Only a few days after this conversation, Alya and Moor fell ill with scarlet fever. Anastasia postponed her return to Sorrento – in part because she did not want to worry Gorky with the threat of infection, since his daughter had died of the disease in 1906. Her decision was fortunate. Marina soon needed help badly. As the two sisters struggled to nurse the sick children, they drew closer together; and when the children slept, Marina confessed freely that she now felt her life was stifled by Seryozha's obsession with his friends in the Eurasian movement. All she wanted was to be left alone to write. She rarely had the chance in the daytime, and her strength had faded by the evening. Marina frankly admitted that because she could not cope without her daughter's help, Alya was being denied education. Marina was the main breadwinner for the family. When Anastasia suggested her sister might find more peace in Russia, Marina was too weary even to consider it seriously.

Moor began to recover gradually, although Alya remained ill. Then, just as the family seemed to be returning to normal, Marina herself went down with scarlet fever. At thirty-five, this was a serious matter. Marina had a high fever, and for some days it was by no means clear that she would survive the illness. Seryozha (immune to the disease, in spite of his own physical frailty) could not abandon the only work he had found, and although Alya was back on her feet, Moor still needed attention. Without Anastasia, the family would have gone under. The last memory Anastasia had was of Seryozha's narrow face, his hat raised, and huge kind eyes, and Marina's present of oranges, given just before the train left the station.

TEN

Tsvetayeva's dislike of Paris was becoming fierce. She longed for Prague, a city she had never really broken away from. By December 1927 she was writing to Anna Teskovà:

Soon it will be Christmas. To tell you the truth, I am so exhausted by life, that I feel nothing. Over the years and years (1917 to 1927) my mind and my soul have grown blunt. I have made a surprising observation: it is for feelings one needs time and not for thought . . . A single example: when I am rolling one-and-a-half kilos of fish in flour I can *think* . . . but I can't feel; the smell interferes, the *fish* interferes – each fish separately out of the whole one-and-a-half kilos of them.[98]

There were other pains. Her old lover Rodzevitch and his wife had settled in Paris, and were now part of the same circle as Seryozha and Marina; indeed, they were close neighbours. Tsvetayeva wrote to Anna Teskovà of the unwelcome, uneasy friendship she had struck up with Madame Rodzevitch: 'We go to the cinema. We buy presents together. I for the family, she for him.'[99] On New Year's Day in

1928, a party was held at Tsvetayeva's flat in which presents were distributed. Among the guests were Konstantin and Moussa Rodzevitch, and most of the others were members of the Eurasian movement. Tsvetayeva felt she was an exile even inside her own home.

In 1924, in one of her finest poems, 'An Attempt at Jealousy', she had written of Rodzevitch's marriage with a fine flow of pride, jealousy and hurt:

. . .

> Sated with newness, are you?
>   Now you are grown cold to magic,
> how is your life with an
>   earthly woman, without a sixth
>
> sense? Tell me: are you happy?
>   Not? In a shallow pit? How is
> your life, my love? Is it as
>   hard as mine with another man?[100]

The confidence of that poem sprang from the conviction that she had mattered as fiercely to Rodzevitch as he had mattered to her, and she could not bear to see him coping very well without her. Now she was hurt by daily confrontation with the fact of his own enjoyment of a domesticity that Tsvetayeva herself, for all her efforts, could never offer.

Among the friends at that New Year's Day party was Vera Suvchinsky, who was always shocked by the Efrons' living conditions. She could not understand how anyone could neglect either her person or her flat to the degree that

157

Marina did. She found the stench repellent, and later re-called with aristocratic disgust the layers of grease in the kitchen.

Altogether, Vera was much more sympathetic towards Marina's handsome, soft-natured husband.

Tsvetayeva was in poor health. A series of abcesses had to be lanced and treated with hot compresses. Her financial anxieties, too, worsened in January 1928 when it looked as if her Czech maintenance would stop. Her only hope of earning money lay in finding subscribers for her new book of poems, *After Russia*. In her gloomiest moments she con-sidered returning to the Soviet Union, though she doubted if the Soviet authorities would let her in. And already she had begun bitterly to assess the situation in which 'in Russia I am a poet without books; here I am a poet without readers'.

Once, in a moment of complete frankness, Tsvetayeva spoke to Mark Slonim of her complete loneliness as a woman. She mourned the absence of a great love: 'I have lived forty years, and never had a man who loved me more than anything else in the world.'

As spring came to the Paris of 1928, Tsvetayeva began to feel an old longing to escape the daily round of re-sponsibilities of her family life. A piece of luck brought a visitor from Russia to stay with the family, who offered to pay for her lodgings by helping in the house. For the first time in ten years, Tsvetayeva had spare time.

So it was that in the spring of 1928 Tsvetayeva came to make friends with an eighteen-year-old boy, Nikolai

Gronsky, whose father was one of the editors of the *émigré* paper *Latest News* and whose mother was a sculptor. The young man had some talent for poetry, and was eager to spend long hours walking with Tsvetayeva in the woods and over the hills near Meudon. His love for mountains rather than the sea coast made him particularly congenial to her, and certainly she and her young hiking companion were more than friends. One of the passages in Tsvetayeva's letters to Georgy Ivask (the Estonian critic with whom she began a correspondence in 1933), which refers to her friendship with Gronsky, admits as much:

> You are right. He was of my race.[101]

Whether or not they were lovers is irrelevant; the degree of Tsvetayeva's emotional involvement did not depend upon sexual contact. That she *was* deeply involved emotionally with Gronsky can be seen from the intensity with which she awaited him that summer on the Atlantic coast. At the beginning of August she had gone with her family to the Villa Jacqueline at Pontaillac (near Royan), where there was a community of Russians on holiday, including Peter and Vera Suvchinsky. It was a period of temporary financial respite, partly through the proceeds of a poetry reading given in June, but mainly through generous gifts from Salomea Halpern and D. S. Mirsky. Tsvetayeva remained at Pontaillac until the end of September, even though Seryozha had to go back to Paris much earlier on Eurasianist matters.

Tsvetayeva stayed on because Gronsky had promised to join her. On the first of September, when Tsvetayeva went joyfully down to meet him, he was not at the station. Bitterly disappointed, she returned to find a letter from him apologizing for his broken word and explaining that he had been obliged to stay behind for the sake of his family.

Tsvetayeva knew instinctively that this marked a decisive end to her hopes, though the excuse was not casual. Gronsky was the only child of two people who felt their exile cruelly, and he was the main thread that held their lives together. He had always known as much, but he discovered it literally when he went home to bid them farewell on his way to Pontaillac. There he found his mother on the point of leaving his father, so he placed his suitcase across the door and began to try and talk his mother out of her decision. Six hours later he was able to return to his own garret, knowing that his mother had agreed to stay, but he was never to join Tsvetayeva by the ocean. Gronsky drifted away from her, as she knew he would. The strongest sense of what his young affection had meant to her in the summer of 1928 comes out in a lyric written many years later:

Because once when you were young and bold
you did not leave me to rot alive among
bodies without souls or fall dead among walls
   I will not let you   die altogether

Because, fresh and clean, you took me
out by the hand, to freedom   and brought spring leaves
in bundles into my house   I shall not
let you be grown over with weeds and forgotten.

> And because you met the status of my
> first grey hairs like a son   with pride
> greeting their terror with a child's joy:
> I shall not let you go grey into men's hearts.[102]

Nikolai's parents controlled *Latest News*, which remained one of the few papers interested in publishing Tsvetayeva's poetry, although editorially they preferred to print her earlier work. Even this welcome as a contributor to *Latest News*, however, was soon to end, for reasons quite unconnected to Nikolai.

Mayakovsky visited Paris in 1928, and Tsvetayeva's admiration for his poetry was now to bring her into conflict with her last supporters among the emigrant community. Their personal relationship had never been a close one. But she often recalled meeting him on a deserted Moscow bridge on one of the last days before her departure. She had asked him then what she would say to people abroad, and he had answered, 'That the truth – is here.' Tsvetayeva often thought of his words, and the sight of him as he strode away. This memory of his words recurred, damagingly, in an exchange that was to become celebrated. Mayakovsky gave a reading at the Café Voltaire in Paris in November 1928, and at the end, Tsvetayeva was asked, 'What can you say about Russia after Mayakovsky's reading?' To this she replied, remembering their earlier encounter, 'Strength is over there.' Her words, and their context, were reported in *Eurasia*. The 'strength' to which she referred was the strength of poetry, as well as the strength of spirit that she found missing in the *émigrés* who surrounded her. Yet the *émigrés* chose to interpret her remark politically. *Latest News* (which, by now, played a very important part in the economics of the Efron family) refused to continue to publish her. Ironically, the poems that were due to appear next were those in praise of the White army (*Swan's Encampment*).

Tsvetayeva began work about this time on a long article about the Russian artist Natalya Goncharova, then living in Paris. Tsvetayeva had little understanding of the way she painted, but she was fascinated by Goncharova's complete indifference to public opinion, and her liking for solitude. The fact that she was the great-granddaughter of Pushkin's wife, whose beauty had led to his fatal duel, preoccupied Tsvetayeva in her essay more sharply than the artist's work. Tsvetayeva sat and made notes in the artist's presence as she tried to arrive at an understanding of the innermost workings of what she admired most in Goncharova: her 'enormous I'. The artist was meanwhile working on illustrations for Tsvetayeva's poem *A Peasant*. However, as Tsvetayeva became more and more deeply involved, she recognized the beginnings of a familiar unease. As she wrote to Anna Teskovà: 'I am always ashamed to give more than the other person needs (i.e. more than he can take!).' That trait in her character, which Rodzevitch had feared and which Mark Slonim described as 'a single naked soul', had frightened away yet another friend.

Slonim had begun to be seriously anxious for Tsvetayeva, for he could see that Seryozha was a sick man, as well as a hopelessly weak one. Tsvetayeva's continued affection for the man aroused his respectful bewilderment. And he saw that Seryozha's fatal mix of naïveté and idealism was soon to prove destructive. Rumours had long circulated that Seryozha was not only a Communist, but also an agent of the NKVD. When they reached Tsvetayeva's ears, she simply refused to believe them – even when Professor Nikolai Alekseyev (one of the founders of the Eurasian movement) and several other members of it publicly declared that Seryozha was a Bolshevik. In reaction, Tsvetayeva decided that Alekseyev was a scoundrel; her chief emotion was pain for Seryozha, and with fierce loyalty she insisted that he was the only moral force left in the Eurasian movement.

However, Seryozha had always longed to serve some cause greater than himself, and just as he had once been misled by dreams of loyalty into joining the White army, he had been casting about for some time in search of an equally lofty ideal. For a time, the Eurasian movement had seemed just such a possibility, but this did not last. Now, finally, as he openly threw in his lot with Communism, he gave himself as unreservedly and fanatically to it as he had served earlier causes.

For some years, it had not been easy for Seryozha to preserve his own sense of dignity: he was always seen as 'the husband of Marina Tsvetayeva', and, worse, a financially dependent husband. His own interest in literature had dwindled, and it was years since he had written anything himself. Slonim commented, 'I never noticed any common views and aims. They went their different ways.'[103]

In the autumn of 1929 Seryozha faced a crisis in his mental and physical health. He was no longer earning any money at all. He was dispirited and extremely thin, and tuberculosis had reasserted itself. Medical assistance was essential and to pay for it the entire family was living on credit. Tsvetayeva was determined that Seryozha should be moved from Meudon to the Haute Savoie. He had to go into a sanatorium for three months, and along with this new call upon her resources Tsvetayeva had to face the possibility that her Czech maintenance would end in 1930. Fortunately her friends, chiefly Salomea Halpern, helped out.

In April 1930 Vladimir Mayakovsky killed himself. An obituary of the Soviet poet, contemptuous in tone, written by the *émigré* critic A. Levinson, was published in the French newspaper *Les Nouvelles Littéraires*, and many well-known French and Russian writers and painters wrote in to protest against it. On 12 July a counter-protest appeared that asserted that Mayakovsky had never been a great Russian poet, and this bore the signatures of (among others) Nina Berberova, Ivan Bunin, Zinaida Gippius and Vladislav Khodasevich. Tsvetayeva attached her signature to neither declaration. Her attitude was to be expressed in her magnificent cycle of seven poems to Mayakovsky.

Grief at Mayakovsky's suicide and her quarrel with the *émigré* community, together with Seryozha's illness and her anxieties over money, brought Tsvetayeva to the edge of a breakdown. On 21 April 1930 she wrote to Anna Teskovà: 'The person writing to you is under attack.' She continued to work for her family's survival, and yet she knew very well that she had begun to take a kind of spiritual leave of them. It was not a question of love. The family had all her heart, but the heart, she felt, expanded at the expense of the soul. She was no longer ashamed to write for money. There were to be no more aristocratic refusals. Now she would accept money, readily, because she knew:

Money is my ransom from the hands of editors, publishers, landladies, shopkeepers, patrons; it is my freedom, and my writing desk.

That desk was the taskmaster of Tsvetayeva's soul, and for the rest of her life she submitted to its discipline willingly and without respite.

My desk, most loyal friend
    thank you. You've been with me on
every road I've taken.
    My scar and my protection.

My loaded writing mule.
    Your tough legs have endured
the weight of all my dreams, and
    burdens of piled-up thoughts.

Thank you for   toughening me.
    No worldly joy could pass
your severe looking-glass –
    you blocked the first temptation

and every base desire
    your heavy oak outweighed
lions of hate, elephants
    of spite   you intercepted.

. . .[104]

Seryozha had to stay in the sanatorium for eight months, and in the summer of 1930 Tsvetayeva and the children went to stay close by. Tsvetayeva was able to see him every day. Once a week she walked with Alya and Moor to the neighbouring small town to buy vegetables and meat for the week.

When the family returned together from the Haute Savoie to Meudon on 9 October 1930, work of any kind was difficult to find. Indeed, there was no longer much if any hope of work for Seryozha. It was almost impossible to find employment in a factory even for the completely fit, and although Seryozha had gained about ten pounds, he was still a sick man and dared not tax his strength. The family continued to live on credit. There was not even enough money for the one franc fifteen centimes fare into the centre of Paris.

Tsvetayeva felt unwanted by all her Parisian acquaintances, and there was no one to whom she felt important, as she wrote to Anna Teskovà on 26 February 1931: 'No one needs me here.' The Czech stipend, on which the whole family depended, stopped coming through in 1931 for several months, and by September they were seriously behind with the rent, with no way of finding the money for the next quarter.

As she wrote to Anna Teskovà on 31 August 1931: 'For the poet, everything is a blessing ... except being over-burdened with ordinary life.'

Tsvetayeva usually sent Anna Teskovà New Year's greet-ings, in which she often assessed her own spiritual state. Tsvetayeva's stocktaking was bleak indeed at the opening of 1932 – so bleak that she was tempted to cast her letter into the stove. By 31 March 1932 Tsvetayeva was reduced to moving the whole family to Clamart, where she had been able to find a much cheaper flat. It was cramped, and Tsveta-yeva had to sleep in the kitchen to make room for her desk and her books.

Her health was deteriorating through undernourishment; she was anaemic and losing her hair. One of Tsvetayeva's four remaining literary outlets, *The Will of Russia*, ceased publication on losing its subsidy from the Czech government. There were months when the whole family had only the five francs a day Alya earned by knitting, and they could not have survived without the generosity of friends such as Salomea Halpern and Mark Slonim.

By now, Tsvetayeva's stern absence of self-pity made her contemptuous of human beings who thoughtlessly took solace from ordinary pleasures, particularly good food. In fact many of her poems written in the middle of that decade poked fun at the gourmet's pleasure in food. Before D. S. Mirsky left for the Soviet Union in 1932, he had often been irritated by her refusal to take any interest in the quality of meals bought for her. Tsvetayeva's harshness was in part a justification of her own inability to perform everyday chores briskly. She explained her asceticism in correspondence with the Estonian critic Georgy Ivask, who began to write to her in 1933.

I'd never throw away the tiniest piece of bread. A crust in a dustbin is a monstrosity . . . So people here think I am mean, but I know it is something else. Undemanding, as were my father and my mother; she did not sink to a favourite dish (– generally – a Protestant and a Spartan!) Didn't ever suspect there might be some particular food which was disliked.[105]

Meanwhile, for the first time in her life, she turned from poetry to write prose memoirs of some of the poets to whom she had been close in the past. These included one on Maximilian Voloshin, begun after the news of his death in 1932, and another about Bely who died in 1934. As she wrote to Anna Teskovà from Clamart on 24 November 1933:

Emigration has made a prose writer out of me.[106]

Grief, she might have added, could still bring poetry from her. In 1934 Tsvetayeva was overcome by the death of Nikolai Gronsky, who had been accidentally killed by an underground train. Although Tsvetayeva had stopped seeing the young man well before he died, his father, who was still on the editorial board of *Latest News*, asked her to write a note about his son's poetry. In the six years between the end of their intimate relationship and Gronsky's death, she had met Nikolai only once, in the spring of 1931, and then casually. She undertook the commission readily enough, and was hurt when her essay was rejected by *Latest News* because the parents were dissatisfied by the intimate tone of her article. To honour her grief she gave an evening reading of her article. Possibly through stress, she lost her voice two days beforehand. But it is in her poems for him, *Epitaph*, that we feel Tsvetayeva's unhappiness, and her unwillingness to accept the usual consolations.

. . .

> And I won't exchange you for sand
> and steam. You took me for kin,
> and I won't give you up for a corpse
> and a ghost: a here, and a there.

. . .[107]

Tsvetayeva was badly in need of kinship. Her own family relations were beginning to collapse, as Tsvetayeva began to vex herself with the question of where she ought to live. Everything seemed to be pushing her towards a return to the Soviet Union. In 1931 Prokofiev had visited Tsvetayeva because he wished to set some of her poems to music. Perhaps, after all, she would be welcome if she returned. And yet part of herself did not believe that: 'Here I am unwanted, and there I am *impossible*.'

ELEVEN

Sergei Efron belonged to the Union for the Repatriation of Russians Abroad, a pro-Soviet organization whose avowed aim was to arrange for exiled Russians to return to the Soviet Union. Alya joined too, and Tsvetayeva knew that both of them longed to go back to Russia. Seryozha's application for a passport, however, was not at first successful, and Tsvetayeva was positively relieved that he couldn't go. For her own part, she was determined not to return. In a letter written to Salomea Halpern in 1933 she declared: 'I am definitely not going; yet this would have meant separation, which for all our bickering, would be hard after twenty years of being together.'

She continued to hesitate. Her sister Anastasia was in the Soviet Union, and Tsvetayeva had friends there. Ehrenburg, who visited Paris on several occasions, failed to warn her. He was sorry to see how hard her life was, and well as he knew the dangers that might await the family in the Soviet Union, he may have genuinely thought that their situation could not be any worse there than in Paris.

Tsvetayeva's obstinate reply to Ivask's letters makes it plain that she would never be forced into a political position she did not hold:

... I think you mean that my hatred against the Bolsheviks is too feeble for the *émigrés'* taste? I'll answer; it's *another kind* of hatred. They hate because their estates have been taken away, I – because Boris Pasternak is not allowed to go to his beloved Marburg, and I to my native Moscow.[108]

It was Pasternak who felt most guilt towards her, in the event. There had been a gradual falling-off in their correspondence. It was not that Pasternak had forgotten his friendship with Tsvetayeva, or that his admiration for her poetry had diminished. But he was ill and unhappy; a frightened man, who knew exactly what had been happening in the USSR after the murder of Kirov (which served as a pretext for Stalin's purges) and could not speak of it. He had been in a miserable state of mind since the beginning of the 1930s, when he had done some travelling to gather material for a book about collective farms in the new countryside. On those journeys he found so much unimaginable calamity everywhere that 'the mind could simply not take it in. I fell ill. For a whole year I couldn't sleep.' Pasternak's failure to warn either Tsvetayeva or her family of the dangers they would face on returning was to haunt him for years after her death.

Pasternak arrived in Paris in June 1935 as a delegate to the Communist-sponsored Congress of Writers in Defence of Culture. He might well have avoided a meeting with

171

Tsvetayeva altogether if she had not herself appeared impetuously at his hotel. Even so, and although they met several times afterwards during his stay in Paris, he remained withdrawn, and it was in part a rage at failing to make real contact with him that prompted Tsvetayeva's harsh letter after his departure.

She certainly showed less comprehension of Pasternak's situation than he did of hers. A large delegation of anti-Fascist writers were happy to attend the congress, among them Heinrich Mann, André Gide, Henri Barbusse, Bertolt Brecht, André Malraux and Louis Aragon (as well as Ehrenburg, of course). Pasternak's presence, along with that of Isaak Babel, had been particularly requested by a group of French writers who had approached the Soviet ambassador in Paris. Pasternak's state of terror was, essentially, rational, since he had been forced to leave his wife behind. At one point he tried to whisper to Tsvetayeva, who was part of the audience, 'I didn't dare not to come: Stalin's secretary came to see me, and I was frightened.' But Tsvetayeva had no way of understanding the nature of the menace.

Pasternak received a prolonged ovation when he rose to speak. There was a terrible irony in his description of poetry as 'an organic function of the happiness of men endowed with the blessed gift of rational speech'.

It is much to Pasternak's credit that when Tsvetayeva approached him while he was standing with other members of the Soviet delegation he welcomed her warmly and proudly, and introduced her to the other members of the delegation as 'one of our major Russian poets'. Pasternak also went to Tsvetayeva's house and got to know her son and daughter as well as her husband. Of Seryozha, Pasternak said he was 'a sensitive, charming, utterly steadfast man, whom I came to love as my own brother'. Pasternak wrote this in 1967, when all the facts of Efron's life were available to him; and certainly 'steadfast' is a surprising adjective to apply to Efron's political principles. As a reflection of Seryozha's loyalty to Tsvetayeva, however, it was entirely just.

Pasternak was well aware that Tsvetayeva's family wanted to return to the Soviet Union; by now, Seryozha, Alya and Moor were all sympathetic to Communism as an ideal. Pasternak could see the terrible life that Tsvetayeva had to live in Paris and the impossibility of her functioning there much longer. All this meant that when Tsvetayeva asked Pasternak his opinion he could not bring himself to warn her. As he wrote somewhat euphemistically in *Novy mir* in 1967: 'I did not know what to advise her, and was too much afraid that she and her remarkable family would find life hard and unsettling in Russia. The tragedy that befell the whole family was infinitely greater even than I had feared.' Pasternak knew exactly how unhappy being an exile made Tsvetayeva, and he was not only thinking of her poverty.

In a letter to Anna Teskovà of 2 July 1935, Tsvetayeva makes it clear that Pasternak need not have blamed himself as bitterly as he did. He had spoken of himself as unwell and on the edge of a nervous breakdown; probably he hardly realized Tsvetayeva's state of mind at all. Certainly what she said to Anna Teskovà in that letter suggests as much: 'I will write about the meeting with Pasternak (there *was* a meeting – and what a non-meeting) when you answer me.'

When Pasternak left Paris, he was too ill to return to Russia immediately and spent two days with the Lomonossoff family in London before catching a boat to Leningrad. Tsvetayeva was incredulous that he had not taken a train through Germany to visit his mother, who lived in Munich. The letter that follows shows how little she understood what Pasternak had been through. She had no idea of the pressures upon him, or she could not have suggested, so cruelly, that he ought to 'think less' about himself.

Late October 1935

Dear Boris,

I have put everything aside in order to answer at once.

About you: one cannot, it is true, judge you as a person . . .

I shall never, for the life of me, understand how one can go past one's mother on a train, past twelve years of waiting. And you should not expect your mother to understand. It is the limit of my comprehension, of human comprehension. I am the opposite of you in such things. I would drag the train *myself* to meet her (although perhaps I would have the same fears, and would have as little pleasure in it). One observation of mine is appropriate to *all* who have been close to me – and there have been many of them – they have been infinitely softer than me. Even Rilke wrote to me: '*Du hast recht, doch Du bist hart.*' [You are right, so you are hard.] And that upset me, for I COULD NOT BE OTHERWISE. Now that I can take stock of the past, I see that my apparent harshness was only the form, the contours of reality an essential barrier of self-defence – defence against *your* softness, Rilke, Marcel Proust and Boris Pasternak. For you would withdraw your hand at the last moment and leave me alone to face my own humanity – long after I had made my exit from the family of men. Among you superhumans I was *merely* a human. I know that yours is a superior race, Boris; and it is *my* turn to put my hand on my heart and say: 'It is not you, but I, who is the proletarian.' Rilke died without summoning his wife, his daughter or his mother. Yet they *all* loved him. He was concerned for his *own* soul. When my time comes to die, I shall have no time to think of my soul (or myself). I shall be fully occupied: have my future pall-bearers been fed? have not my relatives ruined themselves arranging it all? And at best – the most egotistical possibility – I hope they haven't plundered my draft work.

I have only ever been myself (my soul) in my notebooks and on solitary roads (which have been rare), for all my life I have been leading a child by the hand. I no longer had anything left for 'softness' in dealing with people. I could manage only social intercourse, service, *useless* sacrifices. A *mother-pelican* is evil because of the system of sustenance that she creates. There you have it.

About *your* softness: you buy yourself off with it. With this hygienic cotton wool you stop up the openings of the wounds that you yourself inflict. Oh you are kind! If you meet somebody, you are *incapable* of being the first to stand up or clear your throat in preparation for goodbyes. You could not thus 'give offence'. You go out 'for some cigarettes' and disappear for good, turning up in Moscow, on the Volhonka, No. 14 – if not further. Robert Schumann *forgot* that he had children, forgot the date, forgot names, forgot facts. He merely asked about the older girls – whether or not they all had such wonderful voices.

But now for your justification: only *such* people can do *such* things. Goethe, too, was one of your kind. He did not go to say goodbye to Schiller, and for X years he did not go to Frankfurt to see his mother. He was saving himself up for *Faust* Part Two or some such thing. And then at the age of seventy-four he fell in love and decided to get married – no longer taking care of his (physical) heart. For in everything you are squanderers ... For you cure yourselves of everything (of yourselves, of the awful superhuman in yourselves, the divine in yourselves) with the simplest medicine – love ...

I myself chose the world of superhumans. Why should I grumble? ... If your mother forgives you, then she is the mother in the medieval poem – do you remember? – the hero ran, and his mother's heart fell from his hands, and he tripped over it: 'Et voici le coeur lui dit: "T'es-tu fait mal, mon petit?"

Well, Boris, be healthy. Think less about yourself. I shall pass on your greetings to Alya and Seryozha. They remember you with great fondness, and they wish you – as I do – good health, good writing, and good rest.

Regards to Tikhonov if you see him ...

M. Ts.[109]

Human compassion always transcended political and economic theories for Tsvetayeva. She drew back from Seryozha's and Alya's political commitment, not from an abstract principle, but out of a distrust of such principles. Alya's enthusiasm for Communism came from her desire to find in her father's ideals of Communism a replacement for her mother's worship of Art. Much more painful to Tsvetayeva was the realization that Moor's loyalty to her was far from absolute. The only person to whom Tsvetayeva could hope to feel truly necessary was her ten-year-old son, and she worried all the more since the limitations on his intelligence were now clear enough. She longed for him to do something worthwhile with his life. He had always been a difficult child, and Slonim now found him rude and spoilt. Much as she adored him, she hated the way he repeated the commonplaces of ideology learned from his father and sister.

Moor's paramount importance to Tsvetayeva was demonstrated in an unlikely context. Some time in 1935 she made the acquaintance of the American heiress Natalie Clifford Barney, who held a celebrated literary salon at 20 rue Jacob. Barney's own writing talents were modest, but she passionately believed in one particular cause: the power of love between women. She herself had appeared as a character in many novels (notably Radclyffe Hall's *Well of Loneliness*), and she inspired Tsvetayeva to write a remarkable essay: 'Letter to an Amazon'. Tsvetayeva had not experienced any lesbian involvement on a par with her relationships with Sophia Parnok and Sonya Holliday since leaving Russia, and she wrote the essay mainly to analyse the quality of her own responses. She had come to feel that female nature itself defeats the power of any longstanding affair between women – not through the need for a man, but through the universal desire for women to have children. Tsvetayeva's observations are most revealing about her own choices. Her own obsessive love for her son was stronger than any other passion she felt; indeed, it can be said that her longest love (that for Seryozha) was a close approximation of a maternal love.

One of her reasons for continuing to hesitate was a fear of the Soviet education system, in which, after school hours, children were pressed to join Pioneer groups and spend little time with their families. Tsvetayeva saw in that the threat of losing all contact with Moor. As she tried to think her situation through, her old superstitious nature reasserted itself and she wrote to Anna Teskovà, 'Do you know, dear Antonovna, of a good fortune teller in Prague? It seems I can't manage without a fortune teller.'[110] She knew instinctively that she would be incapable of 'singing a welcoming address to the great Stalin', even though she had little knowledge of his crimes. She regarded him simply as the chief figure of a banal church, to which she knew she could give no worship.

Her only certainty as she tried to decide which course of action to take was her belief in poetry. Yet the claims she made in that extraordinary, brilliant, often inconsistent essay, 'Art in the Light of Conscience', were very different from those usually made for poetry. Though she called it 'holy', she took as an example a poem by Pushkin that she felt to be deeply blasphemous – 'Feast During the Plague'. At a time when poets were eager to put their art to the service of humanity or the cause of the people, Tsvetayeva coolly maintained that anyone who so wished to serve 'should join the Salvation Army, or something like that – and give up Poetry'. Poetry was outside the control of the will, and approached the condition of dreaming. 'Art in the Light of Conscience' concludes with Tsvetayeva's comment on her own role.

To be a human being is more important, because more needed. The doctor and the priest are more needed than the poet because they are at the deathbed, while we are not. Doctor and priest are humanly more important, all the rest are socially more important. (Whether the social is itself important is another question, which I shall have the right to answer only from an island.) Except for parasites, in all their various forms, everyone is more important than we are.

And knowing this, having put my signature to this while of sound mind and in full possession of my faculties, I assert, no less in possession of my faculties and of sound mind, that I would not exchange my work for any other. Knowing the greater, I do the lesser, this is why there is no forgiveness for me . . . Only such as I will be held responsible at the Judgement Day of Conscience. But if there is a Judgement Day of the Word, at that I am innocent.[111]

Meanwhile Tsvetayeva's desperate loneliness continued, as she went on living with the threat of Seryozha's and Alya's impending departure, feeling all the while drawn in their wake. As she wrote to Anna Teskovà on 29 March 1936, 'I'm already not living here.'

Few new relationships developed in these bleak years. One of the few was with Vera Bunina. Tsvetayeva did not like Bunin himself, whom she found cold, cruel and smug. Towards his wife, however, she felt warmly. Vera Bunina was a friend of Tsvetayeva's half-sister Valeria, and it was possible for Tsvetayeva to share with Vera a whole lost world of pre-revolutionary Russia. Tsvetayeva's dislike of Bunin himself made it all the easier to sympathize with Vera's situation. Notoriously, he had a young mistress called

Galina Kuznetsova, who travelled everywhere with the family, and Vera had chosen to endure the situation calmly. Tsvetayeva found Vera's continuing love for Bunin altogether admirable. Vera understood herself to be indispensable and stayed with Bunin for that reason, like a mother.

It was in 1935 that Tsvetayeva drew closest to Vera Bunina, but as in all her relationships, she showed anxiety over the least imagined slight. Tsvetayeva's letters to Bunina were often roundabout ways of eliciting money as from other powerful friends, although their relationship remained highly charged. The friendship with Bunina faltered that autumn, in Paris, and over the following year the two women drifted apart, without quarrelling.

Another brief but highly emotional attachment was made with the young poet Anatoly Steiger. Tsvetayeva had met him before only as a close friend of many of her old enemies. It is by no means clear why he turned towards her, but she responded to his attention with all the desperate warmth of a passionate nature starved of affection. He was consumptive, had been seriously ill for a long time and was suffering from the loss of a lover who had recently deserted him. Between August and September 1936 he was recovering from an operation in a Berne hospital, and it was from there that he sent Tsvetayeva a book of his poems. In response to his first letter, she wrote not one but many. At first he was grateful. Tsvetayeva, however, wrote him long, difficult letters, with detailed analyses of the nature of sickness, writing and love. Predictably, as he grew stronger, he drew away from her.

Another poetry reading trip to Belgium in 1936 had produced money enough for Tsvetayeva to clothe Moor. This gave her some happiness, yet signs of Moor's developing character distressed her. He was ill-mannered and showed no signs of natural kindness: he thanked the woman who daily set his food before him as 'if he was barking'. Tsvetayeva half-jokingly called him 'a savage', but without much of a smile. She had become aware that she was pitied for his rude behaviour towards her.

So Tsvetayeva reached the end of 1936, ill with 'flu, and only just able to cope with producing a New Year's tree and presents for Moor. Seryozha and Alya were too concerned with their own plans to return to the Soviet Union to be much interested.

Alya received her visa to return to the USSR in March 1937, and began to pack at once. Seryozha spent a great deal of money buying suitable clothing, and Tsvetayeva was too numb with grief to inquire into where so much money was coming from. It was almost as if Alya were getting married. All their acquaintances contributed towards her 'dowry'. She was given a fur coat, linen, sheets, a watch, suitcases, and cigarette lighters. Tsvetayeva herself walked to the Marché aux Puces (the famous Paris flea market) and bought her a gramophone; she also presented her daughter with her own silver bracelet, a brooch, a cameo and a cross.

When the train left, Tsvetayeva felt a great sadness, and as several months passed with no letters she worried desperately. The first letters were, beyond measure, reassuring.

Alya was living with Seryozha's sister, and earning some money, and sounded very satisfied with her situation.

Not all the news from Moscow was good. Alya wrote that Sonyechka – the beautiful girl Sonya Holliday to whom Tsvetayeva had been so attached in the spring and summer of 1919 – was dead. For the whole of the summer Tsvetayeva's mind went back into Moscow 1919, as she tried to recreate the life she had shared with her young friends of the Vakhtangov studio. She had no idea how soon events were going to impose their own shape upon her.

TWELVE

Seryozha's gentle, weak character makes him an unlikely choice as a spy, yet he certainly received money from 'special' Soviet funds marked for espionage and he was certainly implicated in the murder of Ignace Reiss.

Reiss had been a spy for the Soviet Union for twenty years, mainly in Germany. It was in this way that he first came to help Gertrude Schildbach, who arrived in Paris in 1934 as a bona fide refugee from Hitler. Reiss paid the rent for her apartment and used it occasionally for meetings, without involving her in the NKVD in any other way because he thought her too unstable emotionally.

After the trials of the Old Bolsheviks in August 1936 (including Grigori Zinoviev, Leo Kamenev, I. N. Smirnov and others) had ended with the death sentence on all sixteen defendants, there were many important defections from the NKVD in Europe. Among these was Ignace Reiss, then in Paris, who wrote a courageous letter of protest to the Central Committee of the Communist Party and returned his Order of the Red Banner. He and his wife then made for Lausanne, well aware of their peril.

It was there, on the morning of 4 September 1937, that Reiss and his wife met Gertrude Schildbach in a café and were given a box of poisoned chocolates by her. Other agents had been placed in the café to make sure that Schildbach did not break down and warn Reiss of his danger. One of the reasons she put aside her gratitude to Reiss was a young man called Rossi (an NKVD agent), who had made love to her. She was, however, deceived by him, for he was also the lover of another girl, Renata Steiner. Both girls worked for the same organization as Seryozha, but in the case of Renata Steiner, Seryozha himself had recruited her. It is the main piece of evidence linking him to the murder, although Madame Poretsky (Reiss's wife, who survived) claimed that, when Rossi came to fetch Renata, Efron was among those in the car. The French police, who interrogated him extensively, released him for lack of evidence, but most of his friends knew he was implicated now too.

Tsvetayeva was incredulous. She had come to accept Seryozha's commitment to the Soviet cause, though she had no idea that the money he received every month came from the NKVD. When orders from Moscow forced him to take flight abruptly, she was stunned. The very suddenness of his departure was a blow in itself, but it was followed immediately by close questioning by the French Sûreté. This she found altogether bewildering, and even her interrogators quickly grasped that she was totally ignorant of espionage, politics and her husband's activities. Since she did not understand the thread of their accusations, she replied with quotations from Corneille and Racine. At length the police began to have doubts about her sanity and let her go.

Tsvetayeva sobbed violently for days afterwards. Even if she now knew that Seryozha had been taking money from funds earmarked for espionage, she could not believe in his guilt. The *émigré* community, however, made up its mind decisively, and Tsvetayeva knew her isolation from them was now to be complete. She was numb with terror and loneliness.

Tsvetayeva knew she now had no choice except to return to the Soviet Union. She no longer had Seryozha's small stipend, and since his exposure, the *émigré* community were more likely to hound her to death than contribute to her support. When Mark Slonim met Tsvetayeva in October of that year he found her suddenly aged and dried up, even though she was only forty-five. It was the first time Slonim had seen her cry. Moor was not there, and Slonim afterwards remembered her saying quietly, 'I should like to die, but I must live for Moor's sake. Sergei and Alya don't need me any more.'

Between November 1937 and February 1938 Tsvetayeva could write nothing. Even to write a letter to Anna Teskovà took more stamina than she could muster. It was only in May 1938, when Czechoslovakia was menaced with German invasion, that she was roused from her own misery. She wrote to Teskovà:

The whole of Czechoslovakia is one huge human heart beating just as mine does ... The deepest feeling of disgrace I feel is for

France, but it was not the *real* France that was responsible for this betrayal! In the streets and the squares is the whole of the real France . . .[112]

For the first time in her life, Tsvetayeva rejoiced to see Communist demonstrations against the government in the streets. For the first time, too, she read leftist newspapers. Her personal isolation was now total. To show their abhorrence of the Reiss affair, her Russian neighbours forced her to leave her home and move to a cheap hotel at 13 Boulevard Pasteur. It was there she received her first letter from Seryozha.

Soon, too, a postcard from Prague declared that Anna Teskovà was at least still alive. Tsvetayeva wrote back at once, sharply nostalgic for the time, thirteen years before, when she and Moor and Alya had left Prague for Paris. She had begun a poem-cycle of protests against the invasion. Never attached to precious goods, she asked to be sent a necklace of smoky coloured crystal from Prague, which she was to treasure till her death.

The poems that she wrote for Prague at this time arose from her agony of hatred at the violation of the country in which she had felt most happy. She herself said it: 'I think that Czechia is my first such grief. Russia was too great and I was too young.'

> What tears in eyes now
> weeping with anger and love
> Czechoslovakia's tears
> Spain in its own blood

> and what a black mountain
> has blocked the world   from the light.
> It's time – It's time – It's time
> to give back to God   his ticket.
>
>   . . .[113]

The ticket she wishes to return to God refers to the gesture made by Ivan Karamazov, in Dostoevsky's *The Brothers Karamazov*, when he refused the possibility of salvation if it had to be bought with the suffering of a single child.

By 31 May 1939 the decision to leave for the Soviet Union had been made, although Tsvetayeva told very few people about applying for a visa. She began to sell off her things. She spent a long time sorting out her notebooks. The rest of her time she used to sew on Moor's buttons. At the beginning of June 1939 she went, with Moor, to say goodbye to Mark Slonim, whose house was one of the very few in which she was still received. With great sadness Tsvetayeva and Slonim recalled the altogether carefree days they had once spent together in Prague. Tsvetayeva read to him her latest poem, 'The Bus', which Slonim found particularly brilliant, both in language and humour. It was a long poem, of great virtuosity, as can be seen in its opening lines:

> The bus jumped, like a brazen
> evil spirit,   a demon
> cutting across the traffic
> in streets as cramped as footnotes,
> it rushed on its way   shaking
> like a concert-hall vibrating
> with applause. And we shook in it!

> Demons too. Have you seen
> seeds under a tap? We were
> like peas in boiling soup,
> or Easter toys dancing in
> alcohol. Mortared grain!
> Teeth in a chilled mouth.
> . . .[114]

The poem bored Moor. When he listened to his mother's anxieties about what she would find in Moscow, the yawning thirteen-year-old rebuked her: 'Really, Mama, you won't believe it, but everything will be splendid!' Tsvetayeva and Slonim talked until midnight, even though Moor tried to hurry his mother away. When at last they said goodbye on the landing, Slonim sadly and silently watched them enter the lift. As it began to move, their faces dived down beneath him and disappeared from his sight, and he had a premonition it would be for ever.

There was at least one letter from Seryozha during Tsvetayeva's final months in Paris, and in it he complained of nothing more than a nostalgia for the French cinema. Tsvetayeva herself was numb. In the last weeks before her departure she consoled herself by remembering the much-loved countryside of the land to which she was returning after so long: the juniper tree, the rowanberry and the pine trees she had long missed. And noted in her journal: 'There was one comfort: it was all unstoppable, unchangeable, fatal.'

Tsvetayeva and her son left Paris on 15 June 1939. While waiting for the train to Le Havre to start, she began a letter to Teskovà:

Dear Anna Antonovna!

(I am writing on my palm, that's why the childish hand-writing.)
This is a huge station with green windows – a frightening green
garden – what doesn't grow there! At parting, Moor and I sat for a
while, according to the old custom; we crossed ourselves before the
empty spot where had hung the icon which has lived and travelled
with me since 1918; well, we have to part with everything some
time totally! This is a lesson so that later on to give up everything
won't be frightening, perhaps even not strange . . . A seventeen-
year life is ending. How happy I was at that time. But the happiest
period of my life – remember this – was Mokropsy, Vshenory; and
also my very own mountain. It's strange – yesterday, on the street
I met the hero of that mountain [Rodzevitch], whom I have not
seen for years; he clasped his arms through Moor's arm and mine,
he walked in between us as if it was the most natural thing . . . I
have constantly been meeting everyone. (Right now, I hear, re-
soundingly and threateningly: *express de Vienne* . . . and I remember
the towers and bridges which I will never see.) They are yelling '*En
voiture, madame!*' – as if to me, taking me away from all sorts of
places in my life . . .

We have passed Ractedale [point of no return]! – I will await
news from all of you, give my warm regards to the whole family, I
wish you all health, courage and a long life. I dream of a meeting
in your native land which is more native to me than my own. I
turn around at the sound of it as if it were my own name. Now
everything is already easy; now it is already faint. I embrace you
and kiss each one of you separately and all of you together. I love
you and admire you. I believe in you as in myself.[115]

THIRTEEN

After Tsvetayeva had left Paris, rumours began to reach *émigrés* there that Seryozha was already dead, but in fact both Seryozha and Alya (now pregnant by and living with a man nicknamed Mulia) were at liberty when Tsvetayeva arrived in Moscow. For two months the whole family lived together in a small house in the village of Bolshevo near Moscow. Alya had a job at the Society for Cultural Relations with Foreign Countries, and Seryozha drew a small salary for earlier services rendered to the Soviet state. However, from the first, Seryozha was ill, and Tsvetayeva's notebook suggests that his weakness appalled her, even though she took on the harness of his support as usual.

To the *dacha*. Rendezvous with Seryozha, who is ill. Out for kerosene. S. buys apples. Slowly worsening heart-ache. Ordeal by telephone. Alya enigmatic, for all her apparent cheerfulness. (All this is for my own, and nobody else's, recollection. Moor will not understand it, even if he ever reads it. Nor, indeed, *will* he read it, for he avoids such things.) Cakes, pineapples – things are no easier here for those. Walks with Lilya [Seryozha's sister]. My loneliness.

Washing up, water and tears. The overtone and undertone of everything is horror. Promises of a partition [in the flat] – and the days go by. And the usual wooden scenery – absence of stone, of firm foundations. S.'s illness. Fear of his inner fear. Snippets of his life without me; I have no time to listen; my hands are full; a strain to listen. The cellar: 100 times a day. When can I write?[116]

The sense of Tsvetayeva's continuing loneliness, even as she was reunited with two of those she loved most, is heartbreaking. Her sister Anastasia was already sentenced to imprisonment in a camp, and Moor took little interest in his mother. Even those first two months of hope came to an end with Alya's sudden arrest in August 1939. The last happy memory Tsvetayeva had of her daughter was seeing her in a red Czech dress, a present that Tsvetayeva had brought with her. Four days later Alya was forcibly taken away, the charge of espionage against her serious enough to bring her a sentence of fifteen years. Tsvetayeva noted Alya's departure in her journal:

I: What's the matter, Alya? Why don't you say goodbye to anybody? She looked over her shoulder, in tears – and shrugged.[117]

Approximately a month later, Seryozha was arrested as well. The parting left Tsvetayeva frantic. In her grief, she found it difficult to turn to friends.

Tsvetayeva's meeting with Pasternak after she returned was predictably disappointing. Perhaps this was because both of them were exhausted by their own problems. Pasternak's were of a different kind; he now had a second family and found the threat of any emotional disturbance terrifying. Tsvetayeva, after their long romance by correspondence, was bound to make emotional demands he could neither satisfy nor disappoint.

Pasternak was always pained to recall how inadequately he had behaved, and when his later mistress Olga Ivinskaya teased him with the malicious suggestion 'You should have married Marina', he denied any such wish vehemently. He knew he had failed her by refusing the kind of intimacy she must have been expecting.

Tsvetayeva and Pasternak were humanly very different. Yevgeny, Pasternak's son, still remembers Tsvetayeva's visit to their house when he was about seventeen, and he identifies the difference between the two poets as their attitude towards ordinary, domestic life. The daily round was always to be a burden to Tsvetayeva, while for Pasternak it was the source of endless delight.

Nevertheless, he did many things to make her situation easier. He presented Tsvetayeva to the editor Victor Goltsev, who offered her the task of translating Georgian poets, and poets writing in Yiddish, using literal versions. For this she received payment without having to wait for publication. It was not work she enjoyed, but some of her translations of French poetry, notably Baudelaire, were very fine.

Once Seryozha was arrested, however, Tsvetayeva no longer had a place to live. For a time she and Moor stayed in a small room belonging to Seryozha's sister Elizaveta Efron, then she moved briefly to Merzlik Street. Everywhere was temporary. Pasternak made some effort to find her a place to live, and even went to see Alexander Fadeyev in Peredelkino* (Fadeyev was at that time the head of the Writers' Union); though nothing came of this, Tsvetayeva was sufficiently desperate to risk approaching Fadeyev herself. His reply was cool (without 'dear' or 'esteemed' at the opening, and with no salutation at the end), and though he was not altogether unhelpful, he could offer very little of any practical value.

Tsvetayeva reflected on her own nature, which everyone had found almost inhumanly strong.

About myself. Everybody considers me possessed of manly courage. I know nobody more timid than I. I fear everything: eyes, blackness, footsteps and, most of all, myself, my own head (if it is indeed my head that serves me so devotedly in my notebooks, yet murders me in real life). Nobody knows, nobody sees; it is already a year (approximately) that my eyes have been searching for a hook. But there are no hooks, for everywhere is electricity. No 'candelabras' . . .

For a year I have been taking the measure of death. Everything is ugly and terrifying. You swallow – scum; you leap – hostility, the innate repulsiveness of water. I don't want to confuse things (posthumously). It seems to me that I already, posthumously, fear myself. I do not want to die. I want not to be.

Rubbish. So long as I am needed . . . but, Lord knows, how small I am, how incapable of anything! To live out, to chew out, my time. The bitter absinth.[118]

*A village not far from Moscow where writers were given *dachas* by the State. Pasternak himself had one there.

Tsvetayeva's need to be needed had only Moor on which to focus now, and he gave little sign of any such need. It was for his sake that she lived outside Moscow, in order to be able to take him to and from the local Golitzino School. She hated to leave him there every day, and her main desire on arriving in Moscow was to get out of it again. She still had no window, nor table. And (a terrible restriction for Tsvetayeva) the rules forbade smoking. The first six months of 1940 were a nightmare of loneliness and grief.

But soon Tsvetayeva's material situation deteriorated even further. She had to leave the Writers' Union Club at Golitzino, and she moved to a poor room in Moscow where the cooking facilities were so minimal that she had to make do with only two small saucepans. There was nowhere to keep even the mounds of literal versions from which she worked.

Many old friends were dead. One of these was Osip Mandelstam, whose widow Nadezhda was living in the provinces. Akhmatova, however, was able to meet Tsvetayeva in 1940. Her situation inside the Soviet Union had been every bit as grim as Tsvetayeva's was now – for example, Stalin had held her son as hostage in prison for many years. Nevertheless, unexpectedly, in 1940 the ban against the publication of Akhmatova's poems was lifted. She was staying in Moscow with the Ardov family when Pasternak telephoned to say that Tsvetayeva wanted to meet her.

In her handbag Akhmatova had carried everywhere a manuscript of the cycle of poems that Tsvetayeva had written for her in 1916. She herself had written a poem to Tsvetayeva a few months before they finally met, in which she imagined the two of them walking through the wintry streets of Moscow. In response to Pasternak's call, Akhmatova telephoned Tsvetayeva at once to arrange a meeting. The conversation was brief. When Akhmatova asked if she should come to her, Tsvetayeva answered simply: 'It would be better if I come to you.' Viktor Ardov let Tsvetayeva in, but did not have to introduce his two guests. They greeted each other without the usual platitudes, simply pressing each other's hand. Then the two poets went into a tiny room and remained there alone together for the best part of the day. Akhmatova never spoke fully of what they discussed, but she said that Tsvetayeva had turned out to be a perfectly normal person deeply concerned about her family's fate. And since she knew as well as anyone that the recently published selection did not contain her best work, she may well have shown Tsvetayeva her great poems from *Requiem*.

Tsvetayeva telephoned the next day. Akhmatova suggested that they meet at her friend Nikolay Khardzhiyev's. They sat in his house, talking and drinking wine. Tsvetayeva had recovered her spirits and talked brilliantly, her conversation full of Paris. Akhmatova told Khardzhiyev later that she felt herself to be dull and cow-like in contrast, but he, seeing her opposite the quicksilver Tsvetayeva, was struck by Akhmatova's strength. They left Khardzhiyev's house together, and as they walked along the streets, someone stepped out of the shadows and began to follow them. Akhmatova wondered, 'Her or me?' Akhmatova's sense of a special bond between herself, Mandelstam and Tsvetayeva added a new and tragic dimension to her own sufferings.

When she wrote of Tsvetayeva many years after her death, Akhmatova called her 'Marina the martyr'.

It had cost Tsvetayeva a great deal of nervous energy that day in Khardzhiyev's house to rouse her flagging courage, in circumstances such as she described on 31 August 1940:

My life goes very badly. My non-life. Yesterday I moved out of Ulitsa Gertsena, where we lived very well, and into a tiny temporarily vacant room on the Perzlyakovsky Pereulok. We left all our stuff . . . It can stay until the 15 September . . .

In a word, Moscow has no room for me.

I have nobody to blame. Nor do I blame myself, because such has been my fate. Only – how will it end??

I have written my all. I could, of course, have written more, but I can happily *not* write. Incidentally, I have translated nothing now for over a month. I simply do not touch a notebook. Customs, baggage, sales, gifts (something for everybody), chasing up advertisements (I have already placed four of them, and *nothing* has come of it), family, moving . . . When will it stop?

All right, so it is not only me . . . Agreed, but my father set up the Museum of Fine Arts – the only one in the whole country. He was a founder and a collector; he put in fourteen years of hard work. I say nothing of myself; to quote Chenier's last words: '. . . *et pourtant, il y avait quelque chose là* . . . (pointing to his forehead)'.

I do have friends, but they are powerless. And complete strangers begin to pity me (that embarrasses me, and sets me thinking). That is the worst thing of all, because at the slightest kind word or inflexion I dissolve into tears, like a rock under a waterfall. And

Moor gets furious. He does not understand. It is not a woman crying, but a rock . . .

Moor has started at a good school. He has just been at the parade, and tomorrow he has his first day of classes.

With these changes of abode, I gradually lose my sense of reality. I am slowly being whittled away, a little like that flock that leaves scraps of fleece on every fence. Only my basic *negative* remains.

One more thing, I have a very cheerful nature. (Perhaps that is not it, but there is no other word.) I used to need *very* little in order to be happy. My own *table*. The health of my family. Any weather. And freedom. That is all. And now – such effort to achieve this miserable happiness; it's not just cruel; it's stupid. Life should rejoice in the happy man, should encourage him in this *rare* gift. Because it is from that happy man that happiness flows. It used to flow from me. It used to flow like anything. I used to play with the accumulated burdens of others, like an athlete with his training-weights. Freedom used to flow from me. A person knew, deep down, that, if he threw himself out of the window, he would fall *upwards*. Through me people used to come to life, like the amber. They themselves began to play. It is not my role to be the rocks under the waterfall; rocks which *fall*, together with the waterfall, on to (the conscience of) a person . . . I am moved and upset by the efforts of my friends. I am ashamed – that I am still alive.

It is wise old centenarians who are supposed to feel this way. Were I ten – no, five! – years younger, part of this burden would be removed from my *pride* by that which we shall call, for the sake of brevity, feminine charm. (I speak of my male friends.) But as it is, I, with my grey hair, have absolutely no illusions; everything that people do for me, they do *for me*, not for themselves . . . And that is painful. I had become so used to *giving*!

. . . My problem is that I have nothing external; all heart and fate.

Greetings to your wonderful, quiet surroundings. I have had no summer, but I do not regret it. The only Russian quality in me is my conscience, and it would not have allowed me to enjoy the air, the silence, the blue, knowing and never for a moment forgetting that at the same instant somebody else was suffocating in the heat and the stones.

That would be an excess torture.

The summer went well. I made friends with an eighty-four-year-old nanny, who has lived in this family for sixty years. And there was a *wonderful* cat – mouse-coloured and Egyptian, long-legged; a monster, a monster, but divine. I would give my soul for such a nanny and such a cat.

Tomorrow I shall go to the Litfond ('and many, many times more') to check about a room. I don't have faith. Write to me at Merzlyakovsky Pereulok, c/o Elizaveta Yakovlevna Efron.

I am not registered here, so better not to write to me direct.

Embraces. Heartfelt thanks for remembering me. Warm greetings to Ilya Grigoryevich.

M. Ts.[119]

Pavel Antokolsky, a friend from her days of theatrical excitement, was living in Moscow. He preferred to see very little of Tsvetayeva. When I talked about her to him thirty-five years later, he spoke of a group of friends who sustained her, among them Arseny Tarkovsky, a poet-translator. He spoke of a woman aged through fatigue and grief. He was shocked by the change in her physical appearance. He had met her once in the intervening years in 1928 in Paris, when she had sat with him in the Boulevard St Michel, and had found her slimmer and greyer, but still beautiful. He described a reading held at Victor Goltzev's house. Tsvetayeva read in a timid voice unlike her own, and seemed remote from the audience. Altogether, Antokolsky's description of her suggests someone whose anxiety was preoccupying her beyond the point where ordinary human relationships were possible – as Antokolsky put it: *'Elle est autre.'* He also commented on the formal, if not overtly hostile, relationship she had with her son Moor, who customarily addressed her as *'vous'*. Antokolsky heard him that very evening blame his mother's behaviour for their situation.

Moving, as she had to, from place to place, Tsvetayeva was now in a state of continual panic. In jottings in the margins of her rough notebook, dated 24 January 1940, she wrote:

A new uncomfortable house – again I cannot sleep at nights. I am afraid – too much *glass* – too much solitude – night sounds and fears; a car (God knows why it's moving); a stray cat, the crackle of wood – I jump up – snuggle up close to Moor on his bed (without waking him) – and again I read . . . and again jump up and so, to daybreak.[120]

In the summer of 1940 the Nazi–Soviet pact shattered many believing Communists. Tsvetayeva was too weary to respond with astonishment. From her husband and her daughter, she had heard nothing for months. She stood in line with others in an attempt to deliver food parcels to Seryozha in prison, but there was no sign of what was happening to him. She wrote many letters to Alya.

When Tsvetayeva at last received a letter from her daughter, she was overwhelmed with joy to have evidence that Alya was still alive and to have something positive she could do to help. Her letter to Alya is worth quoting in its entirety.

Moscow, 12 April 1941
Saturday

Dear Alya,

At last, your first letter – in a blue envelope, dated the 4th. I stared at it from 9 a.m. to 3 p.m. when Moor came home from school. It lay on his dinner-plate, and he saw it as soon as he opened the door; and with a contented and even self-satisfied 'A-ah!' – pounced on it. He would not let me read it. Both his own letter and mine he read aloud. But even before the reading, I sent you a postcard. I couldn't wait. That was yesterday, the 11th. And on the 10th I took in a parcel and they accepted it.

I have been industriously at work finding provisions for you, Alya. I already have sugar and cocoa; I am about to have a shot at lard and cheese – the most solid I can find. I shall send you a bag of dried carrots; I dried them in the autumn on all the radiators. You can boil them. At least they are still vegetables. It is a pity, though not unnatural, that you do not eat garlic. I have a whole kilo stored up just in case. But bear in mind that raw potato is a reliable and less unpleasant method. It is effective as lemon – that I know for certain.*

I have already told you that your belongings are free. I myself was given the job of unlocking them – so we shall rescue everything. Incidentally, the moths have eaten nothing. All your things are intact – books, toys and a lot of photographs. I took for myself

*Against diseases of vitamin deficiency.

some kind of bark box, and I keep my beads in it. Should I, perhaps, send you the silver and turquoise bracelet for your other hand? You can wear it without taking it off; it is even difficult to take off. And perhaps one of the rings? Please answer these questions. Which blankets? (Your spare blue one got lost at Bolshov together with many others, none of them yours.) I have: my colourful knitted one (big, but not heavy; warm); your father's beige plaid (small), and the dark blue Spanish shawl. I would still take the knitted one, with the shawl to follow next time (it is yours, after all). I shall also send naphthalene. The sacks are ready. There are also two dresses – one austere, and the other more decorative; we shall adjust the sleeves. Mulia swears he will get oil of cloves for the mosquitoes. A wonderful smell – one I have worshipped since my childhood. And there will be a lot of bits and pieces for presents.

Spring is still fairly fresh here. The ice is not yet breaking up. Yesterday the cleaning lady brought me a gift of pussy willow branch. And in the evening (I have a huge window, the width of the whole wall) I looked through it at the big yellow moon, and the moon looked back through it to me. With a fresh-skinned willow branch one feels fresh-skinned oneself – very fresh-skinned! Moor said to me just now in indignation: 'Mama, you look like an awful old village hag!' And I was very pleased that he said a 'village' one. Poor Puss! He so loves beauty and order, and our room is like the one on Boris and Gleb Street – too many things, all piled up on top of each other. His main joy is the radio, which, for some unknown reason, has started broadcasting absolutely everything. I recently heard Eva Curie from America. Alya, among my treasures (I'm writing nonsensically), I preserve your moustach-ioed gingerbread cat. Kiss Red for me – a good cat. I shall never have another cat. After that one of yours climbed into Nikolka's cradle. I loved it madly, and it was terrible to part with it. It has remained like a nail in my heart.

I am finishing my free verse Russian Jews. I translate every day. The main difficulty is the incoherence, imprecision and lack of motivation of the images. Everything falls to pieces. The glue and the seams show all over the place. Some of them write no rhyme or measure. It seems that after the Russian Jews will come the Balts. I write nothing of my own. No time. A lot of housework. The cleaning lady comes once a week.

I also re-read Leskov – last winter in Golitzino. And I read Benvenuto in Goethe's translation when I was seventeen. I particularly remember the salamander and the slap.

I visited Nina a few times over the winter. She is constantly unwell, but she works, whenever she is able, and is happy in it. I gave her a short artificial fur jacket – she really had frozen to death – and, for her birthday, one of my metal cups, from which nobody drinks except her and me.

I want to send this off now, so I shall finish. Keep strong and alert. I hope that Mulia's trip is only a matter of time. I have recently been admitted to the Grupkom of Goslitizdat – unanimous. So you see, I am trying.

Keep well. Kisses . . .

Moor is writing to you himself.

Mama[121]

For all the courage and optimism this letter suggests, Tsvetayeva had lost hope soon after her return to the Soviet Union and was by now convinced that she was 'condemned to write as a wolf howls whatever system I live under'. By 10 June her telephone had stopped working and there was a move to a new *dacha* in the offing. However, all plans were overwhelmed by the single fact of the German invasion. Her situation worsened at once. From being a lonely, unhappy creature with a suspect past, she was abruptly transformed into a potential spy. Her early writings in praise of Germany and German literature were scrutinized as political statements.

Shortly afterwards, Tsvetayeva had her first and only encounter with the one friend who had been powerfully placed in the Soviet hierarchy all that time – Ilya Ehrenburg. Ehrenburg himself described his encounter with Tsvetayeva soon after the invasion as disappointing to both of them. He said frankly:

> The meeting was a failure through my fault. My thoughts were far away (understandably perhaps, since the news was all of retreats then). Marina sensed it at once and gave our conversation the flavour of a business interview. She had come, she said, to seek my advice about translating and other matters.[122]

Tsvetayeva was by now anxious for the fifteen-year-old Moor, who had been put in a fire-watching squad with the task of throwing fire-bombs off the roof of the high apartment building where she had rented a tiny room on the top floor. Tsvetayeva went to see Pasternak to ask his advice about how she could help Moor and explained that she had formed the idea of going off to the Tartar region, where she knew several other Union writers had been evacuated; she was eager to leave Moscow because of the rising suspicion of her on every side. Pasternak tried to dissuade her from leaving, but he did not offer (as he well might have done) a place to stay with him at Peredelkino. So it was that she undertook, fatefully, her own evacuation.

Pasternak saw Tsvetayeva and Moor off at River Fort on the outskirts of Moscow, from where it was possible to go by steamer to Chistopol and other towns on the river Kama. This farewell was to be their last.

FOURTEEN

For ten days in August 1941, Tsvetayeva stayed as an evacuee from Moscow with the Bredelshikovs in Yelabuga. It was a quiet, small house. Tsvetayeva shared a room with Moor. Their window looked over meadows. Her peasant hosts had never heard of her. All they saw were her dark dress, her old brown coat and the lines of fatigue in her face. They could not help laughing at her knitted pea-green beret and the large apron she wore in the house, and found there was something witch-like about her thin, stooping figure.

Yelabuga was a small town in the Tartar Autonymous Republic and contained few wealthy people. Tsvetayeva was unlikely to find anyone who wanted to buy the silver she had brought with her; nevertheless, she carried it about everywhere in search of a purchaser. In the evening she was too exhausted to cook; she and Moor ate in the local wartime canteen.

Writers acceptable to the state had been evacuated to Chistopol on the other side of the river Kama, a three-day journey away, and she decided to make a last attempt to join, to beg any work, suitable or not. An earlier letter to the President of the Tartar Writers' Union, asking for work as a translator, had been ignored. Even permission to work in the kitchen, however, was refused. Nikolai Aseev, who was in charge of allocating living space, had abstained when the committee voted on the matter and refused to arrange for her to stay; and even refused to lend her any money. After their last conversation she sat for a long time on a bench near the river, absorbing the finality of his rejection.

She returned from this journey so bleak and weary that she did not even have the heart to clean the fish Bredelshikov had caught, still less fry it. Anastasia Ivanovna Bredelshikova did it for her; in the same spirit, she had earlier showed her how to roll home-grown cigarettes. They often smoked together, without talking much. Now Tsvetayeva's silence was bitter. She saw in Moor's sullen face no welcome, rather a continuing hostility. He was a gawky boy, too big for his clothes and too strong for his age. People in the street sometimes asked why he wasn't in uniform. For this, he blamed Tsvetayeva.

On Saturday, 30 August, he could be heard quarrelling violently with her. He reproached her for a lifetime of irresponsibility, which had led to the imprisonment of his father and the sentence of forced labour passed on his sister. Tsvetayeva's voice rose too, but she seemed to be pleading rather than angry and she made no attempt to rebut his charges. She continued to call him by his pet name.

The following day, all the inhabitants of Yelabuga were supposed to help in the preparation of an airstrip; everyone who turned up was given a loaf of bread. Anastasia Ivanovna Bredelshikova went along with Moor, while her husband and grandson went off fishing. Tsvetayeva seemed preoccupied. She did not mind being left alone.

She no longer understood what she was struggling for. All her life she had survived because she had known that she was needed. Now Moor's resentment had destroyed any belief in her own worth.

Her material situation was not yet alarming. She had over 400 roubles and, more valuable, stocks of semolina, sugar and rice. There was even the remains of a pan of cooked fish. She knew herself to be one of the greatest European poets of the century. But her inner loneliness was now complete.

No one can know with certainty what decided her to give up at this particular moment. Not long before, she had noted: 'I am, at the moment, dead. I do not, at the moment, exist; I do not know whether I shall exist some time in the future.'

If Stalin saw no sense in wasting resources on evacuating prisoners from the Lubianka, Seryozha would already have been shot. Tsvetayeva must have heard rumours of that possibility. And so, as she found the nail used to tether horses, and attached a hempen rope to it, she may, in thought, have been following Seryozha once again.

Seryozha was shot in Lubianka prison. Alya, who also spent the first two years of her sentence there, lost her baby as a result of savage beatings. She was transferred in 1941 to a labour camp in the Turukhansky region, where she was sentenced to an additional ten years. She did not serve this in full, however. Pasternak (who had exchanged letters with her) and Ivinskaya took her in upon her release in 1955 after sixteen years' imprisonment and looked after her until she recovered her health. She stayed with them throughout the period when Pasternak himself came under most attack, and she later moved to a house in Tarusa, her mother's childhood home. There Alya devoted the rest of her life to arranging and preserving her mother's archives, and seeing her work into print when it became possible. She published her brilliantly observant recollections of her mother before she died, of a heart attack, in 1975.

Moor did not go to his mother's funeral, and if he felt grief for her, he showed it to no one. Akhmatova, who looked after Moor with great kindness after Tsvetayeva's death, noted his coldness towards his mother's memory. This is all the sadder since it may well have been to free the son from the burden of her ostracism that Tsvetayeva took her life when she did. If so, the gesture was wasted. Moor quickly enlisted in the army and died later in the battle for Moscow.

Anastasia spent the years 1938–40 in Siberia, and had no chance to see her sister after the latter's return to the Soviet Union. A volume of her memoirs of her sister was published in Moscow in 1971. She is at present in a Writers' Rest Home outside Moscow.

To the end of their lives, the thought of Marina's death continued to haunt all those who had known her. Pasternak mourned its arbitrary timing, for he felt, with some guilt, that if she had only been able to hold out for another month, he might have been able to find her a billet in Chistopol itself. Anna Akhmatova had no chance to give Marina the poem composed in her honour, in return for so many poems dedicated to herself. She kept a photograph of Tsvetayeva, together with one of her own, because both showed them wearing the same brooch, which Tsvetayeva had given her. When comparisons were made in literary articles between the two poets, Akhmatova was suspicious of their being put together mainly because they were women. For her own part, she preferred to set both Tsvetayeva's name and her own alongside Pasternak and Mandelstam in a grand fellowship of tragic equals.

1. Ariadne Efron, *Stranitsy vospominanii*, Paris, 1979, p. 36.

2. Letter from Marina Tsvetayeva to Boris Pasternak, late October 1935, *Novy mir*, No. 4, 1969.

3. Letter from Tsvetayeva to Pasternak, 10 July 1926, *Neizdannye pisma*, Paris, 1972.

4. Marina Tsvetayeva, 'Art in the Light of Conscience', trans. Angela Livingstone and Valentina Coe, in *Modern Russian Poets on Poetry*, Ann Arbor, 1974.

5. 'My Pushkin', in Marina Tsvetayeva, *A Captive Spirit: Selected Prose*, ed. and trans. Janet Marin King, Ann Arbor, 1980, p. 321.

6. 'Mother and Music', in Tsvetayeva, *A Captive Spirit*.

7. 'The House at Old Pimen', in Tsvetayeva, *A Captive Spirit*, p. 233.

8. From Osip Mandelstam's poem 'To the German Tongue', 1932.

9. 'My Pushkin', in Tsvetayeva, *A Captive Spirit*, p. 335.

10. ibid., p. 288.

11. 'The Flagellant Nuns', in *Pages from Tarusa*, ed. Andrew Field, Boston, 1964.

12. 'Mother and Music', in Tsvetayeva, *A Captive Spirit*, p. 292.

13. Anastasia Tsvetayeva, *Vospominaniya*, Moscow, 1971, 1974 and 1983, p. 109.

14. 'Mother and Music', in Tsvetayeva, *A Captive Spirit*, p. 293.

15. ibid.

16. As quoted in A. Tsvetayeva, *Vospominaniya*, p. 300.

17. Tsvetayeva, *A Captive Spirit*, p. 107.

18. Gumilyov, *Appollon*, V, St Petersburg, 1911. As quoted in Simon Karlinsky, *Marina Cvetayeva, Her Life and Art*, Berkeley, 1965.

19. 'A Living Word About a Living Man', in Tsvetayeva, *A Captive Spirit*.

20. Efron, *Stranitsy vospominanii*, p. 29.

21. ibid., p. 30.

22. Marina Tsvetayeva, *Selected Poems*, ed. and trans. Elaine Feinstein, London, 1986, p. 76.

23. Tsvetayeva, *A Captive Spirit*, p. 170.

24. Tsvetayeva, *Selected Poems*, p. 73.

25. ibid., pp. 74–5.

26. *Selected Poems of Osip Mandelstam*, ed. and trans. James Greene, London, 1980.

27. Nadezhda Mandelstam, *Hope Against Hope*, trans. Max Hayward, London, 1971, p. 460.

28. Tsvetayeva, *Selected Poems*, p. 11.

29. ibid., p. 25.

30. 'A Living Word About a Living Man', in Tsvetayeva, *A Captive Spirit*, p. 90.

31. Marina Tsvetayeva, 'A Tale of Sonyechka', *Russkie zapiski*, III, 1938.

32. Marina Tsvetayeva, 'A Tale of Sonyechka', Part II (unpublished MS, University of Basel).

33. 'A Tale of Sonyechka', *Russkie zapiski*, p. 43.

34. ibid., p. 44.

35. ibid., p. 60.

36. 'A Tale of Sonyechka', unpublished MS.

37. ibid.

38. Marina Tsvetayeva, 'Dnevniki i zapiski, 1917–1920', *Izbrannaya proza v dvukh tomakh*, New York, 1979, p. 65.

39. ibid., p. 32.

40. Marina Tsvetayeva, *Proza*, New York, 1953, p. 132.

41. Tsvetayeva, 'Dnevniki i zapiski', p. 52.

42. ibid., p. 83.

43. Letter from Tsvetayeva to Anastasia Tsvetayeva, December 1920, in *Neizdannye pisma*, Paris, 1972.

44. ibid.

45. ibid.

46. Tsvetayeva, *Proza*, p. 245.

47. Tsvetayeva, *Selected Poems*, p. 18.

48. Nina Berberova, *The Italics Are Mine*, New York, 1969.

49. Tsvetayeva, letter to Anna Akhmatova, August 1921, in *Neizdannye pisma*.

50. ibid.

51. Quoted in Efron, *Stranitsy vospominanii*, pp. 86–7.

52. Nadezhda Mandelstam, *Hope Abandoned*, trans. Max Hayward, London, 1974, pp. 460–61.

53. Efron, *Stranitsy vospominanii*, p. 75.

54. ibid.

55. ibid., p. 91.

56. Tsvetayeva, *A Captive Spirit*, p. 131.

57. Efron, *Stranitsy vospominanii*, p. 94.

58. ibid.

59. ibid., p. 96.

60. Letter from Pasternak to Tsvetayeva, 13 June 1922, in *Neizdannye pisma*.

61. Letter from Tsvetayeva to Pasternak, 29 June 1922, in *Neizdannye pisma*.

62. Letter from Tsvetayeva to Pasternak, 9 March 1923, in *Neizdannye pisma*.

63. From Marina Tsvetayeva, 'A Poet on Criticism', in Karlinsky and Appel, *The Bitter Air of Exile*, Berkeley, 1977.

64. Letter from Tsvetayeva to Pasternak, 19 November 1922, in *Neizdannye pisma*.

65. Tsvetayeva, *Selected Poems*, p. 28.

66. Letter from Tsvetayeva to Alexander Bakhrakh, in *Mosty*, Munich, Vol. 5, 1960; and Vol. 6, 1961.

67. ibid.

68. ibid.

69. ibid.

70. ibid.

71. ibid.

72. ibid.

73. ibid.

74. Taped interview with Konstantin Rodzevitch, 1976.

75. Tsvetayeva, *Selected Poems*, p. 40.

76. Letter from Sergei Efron, quoted in Efron, *Stranitsy vospominanii*, p. 167.

77. Letter from Tsvetayeva to Bakhrakh, in *Mosty*.

78. Tsvetayeva, *Selected Poems*, p. 68.

79. ibid., p. 48.

80. ibid., p. 59.

81. Letter from Pasternak to Tsvetayeva, 14 June 1924, in *Neizdannye pisma*.

82. Letter from Tsvetayeva to Anna Teskovà, 5 December 1924, in *Pisma k Anne Teskovoi*, Prague, 1969.

83. ibid.

84. ibid.

85. Letter from Tsvetayeva to Pasternak, 19 July 1925, in *Neizdannye pisma*.

86. Letter from Tsvetayeva to Anna Teskovà, 10 October 1925, in *Pisma k Anne Teskovoi*.

87. ibid., 30 December 1925.

88. See 'The Ratcatcher', in Tsvetayeva, *Selected Poems*, p. 78.

89. Pasternak to Tsvetayeva, 20 April 1926, in *Neizdannye pisma*.

90. Elena Izvolskaya, 'O Tsvetavoi', in *Opyty*, No. 3, New York, 1954.

91. Letter from Tsvetayeva to Anna Teskovà, 8 June 1926, in *Pisma k Anne Teskovoi*.

92. Letter from Tsvetayeva to Pasternak, 10 July 1926, in *Neizdannye pisma*.

93. Letter from Tsvetayeva to Pasternak, 21 May 1926, in *Neizdannye pisma*.

94. Letter from Tsvetayeva to Rainer Maria Rilke, in *Letters Summer 1926*, ed. Yevgeny Pasternak, Yelena Pasternak and Konstantin Azadovsky, London, 1986.

95. Letter from Tsvetayeva to Pasternak, 1 January 1927, in *Neizdannye pisma*.

96. ibid.

97. Letter from Tsvetayeva to Anna Teskovà, 21 February 1927, in *Pisma k Anne Teskovoi*.

98. ibid., 12 December 1927.

99. ibid., 3 January 1928.

100. Tsvetayeva, *Selected Poems*, p. 71.

101. Letter from Tsvetayeva to Georgy Ivask, in *Russkii literaturnyi archiv*, ed. Dmitry Chizhevsky and Michael Karpovich, New York, 1956.

102. Tsvetayeva, *Selected Poems*, p. 84.

103. See Mark Slonim, 'O Marine Tsvetayevoi', *Novy zhurnal*, No. 100, 1970; No. 104, 1971.

104. Tsvetayeva, *Selected Poems*, p. 87.

105. Letter from Tsvetayeva to Ivask, in *Russkii literaturnyi archiv.*

106. Letter from Tsvetayeva to Anna Teskovà, 24 November 1933, *Pisma k Anne Teskovoi.*

107. Tsvetayeva, *Selected Poems*, p. 83.

108. Letter from Tsvetayeva to Ivask, 4 April 1933, in *Russki literaturnyi archiv.*

109. Letter from Tsvetayeva to Pasternak, late October 1935, *Novy mir*, 4, 1969.

110. Letter from Tsvetayeva to Anna Teskovà, 15 February 1936 in *Pisma k Anne Teskovoi.*

111. Tsvetayeva, 'Art in the Light of Conscience', in *Modern Russian Poets on Poetry.*

112. Letter from Tsvetayeva to Anna Teskovà, 29 May 1938, in *Pisma k Anne Teskovoi.*

113. Tsvetayeva, *Selected Poems*, p. 99.

114. ibid., p. 91.

115. Letter from Tsvetayeva to Anna Teskovà, in *Pisma k Anne Teskovoi.*

116. Journal notes, in *Neizdannye pisma*, pp. 627–8.

117. ibid, p. 630.

118. ibid.

119. ibid.

120. ibid., pp. 627–8.

121. Tsvetayeva, letter to Ariadne Efron, 12 April 1941, in *Neizdannye pisma.*

122. Ilya Ehrenburg, *People, Years, Life*, vols. 1–6, London, 1961–6.

In Russian

Ariadne Efron, *Stranitsy vospominanii* (*Pages from Memoirs*), Paris, 1979.

Mark Slonim, 'O Marine Tsvetayevoi', *Novy zhurnal*, No. 100, 1970; No. 104, 1971.

Anastasia Tsvetayeva, *Vospominaniya* (*Memoirs*), Moscow, 1971, 1974 and 1983.

Marina Tsvetayeva, *Izbrannye proizvedeniya* (*Selected Works*), ed. Ariadne Efron and Anna Saakiants, Moscow-Leningrad, 1965.

Marina Tsvetayeva, 'Dnevniki i zapiski, 1917–1920', *Izbrannaya proza v dvukh tomakh*, New York, 1979.

Marina Tsvetayeva, *Neizdannye pisma* (*Unpublished Letters*), ed. Gleb and Nikita Struve, Paris, 1972.

Marina Tsvetayeva, *Neizdannoe. Stikhi, teatr, proza* (*Unpublished Works. Poetry, Drama, Prose*), Paris, 1976. (Contains *Juvenilia* and 'A Tale of Sonyechka'.)

Marina Tsvetayeva, *Pisma k Anne Teskovoi* (*Letters to Anna Tesková*), Prague, 1969.

Marina Tsvetayeva, *Proza*, New York, 1953.

Marina Tsvetayeva, 'A Tale of Sonyechka', *Russkie zapiski*, III, 1938.

Marina Tsvetayeva, letters to Alexander Bakhrakh, in *Mosty*, Munich, Vol. 5, 1960, and Vol. 6, 1961.

Marina Tsvetayeva, letters to Roman Gul, in *Novy zhurnal*, No. 58, 1959.

Marina Tsvetayeva, letters to Georgy Ivask, in *Russkii literaturnyi archiv* (*Russian Literary Archives*), ed. Dmitry Chizhevsky and Michael Karpovich, New York, 1956.

Marina Tsvetayeva, letters to Anatoly Steiger, in *Opyty*, Nos. 5, 7 and 8, New York, 1955–7.

Marina Tsvetayeva, excerpts from letters to various persons, ed. Ariadne Efron and Anna Saakiants, published in *Novy mir* No. 4, Moscow, 1969.

Marina Tsvetayeva, *Diaries of 1917–1921*, prepared for publication but published only as articles in periodicals.

In English

Nina Berberova, *The Italics Are Mine*, New York, 1969.

Isaiah Berlin, *Personal Impressions*, London, 1980.

Andrew Field (ed.), *Pages from Tarusa*, Boston, 1964.

Henry Gifford, *Pasternak: A continued study*, Cambridge, 1977.

Alexander Gladkov, *Conversations with Pasternak*, ed. and trans. Max Hayward, London, 1977.

Amanda Haight, *Akhmatova*, Oxford, 1976.

Ronald Hingley, *Nightingale Fever*, London, 1982.

Olga Ivinskaya, *A Captive of Time*, with notes by Max Hayward, London, 1978.

Simon Karlinsky, *Marina Cvetayeva, Her Life and Art*, Berkeley, 1965.

Simon Karlinsky, *Marina Cvetayeva: The Woman, the World and Her Poetry*, Cambridge, 1985.

Letters Summer 1926, ed. Yevgeny Pasternak, Yelena Pasternak and Konstantin M. Azadovsky, London, 1986.

Nadezhda Mandelstam, *Hope Against Hope*, trans. Max Hayward, London, 1971.

Nadezhda Mandelstam, *Hope Abandoned*, trans. Max Hayward, London, 1974.

Osip Mandelstam, *Selected Poems*, ed. and trans. James Greene, London, 1980.

Boris Pasternak, 'Safe Conduct', from *Pasternak, Prose and Poems*, London, 1945.

Marina Tsvetayeva, 'Art in the Light of Conscience', trans. Angela Livingstone and Valentina Coe, in *Modern Russian Poets on Poetry*, Ann Arbor, 1974, pp. 147–84.

Marina Tsvetayeva, *A Captive Spirit: Selected Prose*, ed. and trans. Janet Marin King, Ann Arbor, 1980.

Marina Tsvetayeva, *The Demesne of Swans*, trans. Robin Kemball, 1980.

Marina Tsvetayeva, 'A Downpour of Light', trans. Donald Davie and Angela Livingstone, in *Critical Essays*, London, 1969.

Marina Tsvetayeva: A Pictorial Biography, Ann Arbor, 1980, with an introduction by Carl Proffer.

Marina Tsvetayeva, 'A Poet on Criticism', in Karlinsky and Appel, *The Bitter Air of Exile*, Berkeley, 1977.

Marina Tsvetayeva, *Selected Poems*, ed. and trans. Elaine Feinstein, Oxford, 1971 and 1981 and London, 1986.

In French

Marina Tsvetayeva, *Lettre à mon frère feminin*, Paris, 1979.

Lydia Tchoukovskaia, *Entretiens avec Anna Akhmatova*, Paris, 1980.

FOR THE BEST IN PAPERBACKS, LOOK FOR THE 🐧

In every corner of the world, on every subject under the sun, Penguin represents quality and variety – the very best in publishing today.

For complete information about books available from Penguin – including Pelicans, Puffins, Peregrines and Penguin Classics – and how to order them, write to us at the appropriate address below. Please note that for copyright reasons the selection of books varies from country to country.

In the United Kingdom: Please write to *Dept E.P., Penguin Books Ltd, Harmondsworth, Middlesex, UB7 0DA*

If you have any difficulty in obtaining a title, please send your order with the correct money, plus ten per cent for postage and packaging, to *PO Box No 11, West Drayton, Middlesex*

In the United States: Please write to *Dept BA, Penguin, 299 Murray Hill Parkway, East Rutherford, New Jersey 07073*

In Canada: Please write to *Penguin Books Canada Ltd, 2801 John Street, Markham, Ontario L3R 1B4*

In Australia: Please write to the *Marketing Department, Penguin Books Australia Ltd, P.O. Box 257, Ringwood, Victoria 3134*

In New Zealand: Please write to the *Marketing Department, Penguin Books (NZ) Ltd, Private Bag, Takapuna, Auckland 9*

In India: Please write to *Penguin Overseas Ltd, 706 Eros Apartments, 56 Nehru Place, New Delhi, 110019*

In Holland: Please write to *Penguin Books Nederland B.V., Postbus 195, NL–1380AD Weesp, Netherlands*

In Germany: Please write to *Penguin Books Ltd, Friedrichstrasse 10–12, D–6000 Frankfurt Main 1, Federal Republic of Germany*

In Spain: Please write to *Longman Penguin España, Calle San Nicolas 15, E–28013 Madrid, Spain*

In France: Please write to *Penguin Books Ltd, 39 Rue de Montmorency, F-75003, Paris, France*

In Japan: Please write to *Longman Penguin Japan Co Ltd, Yamaguchi Building, 2–12–9 Kanda Jimbocho, Chiyoda-Ku, Tokyo 101, Japan*

A SELECTION OF FICTION AND NON-FICTION

A Confederacy of Dunces John Kennedy Toole

In this Pulitzer-Prize-winning novel, in the bulky figure of Ignatius J. Reilly, an immortal comic character is born. 'I succumbed, stunned and seduced . . . it is a masterwork of comedy' – *The New York Times*

The Labyrinth of Solitude Octavio Paz

Nine remarkable essays by Mexico's finest living poet: 'A profound and original book . . . with Lowry's *Under the Volcano* and Eisenstein's *Que Viva Mexico!*, *The Labyrinth of Solitude* completes the trinity of masterworks about the spirit of modern Mexico' – *Sunday Times*

Falconer John Cheever

Ezekiel Farragut, fratricide with a heroin habit, comes to Falconer Correctional Facility. His freedom is enclosed, his view curtailed by iron bars. But he is a man, none the less, and the vice, misery and degradation of prison change a man . . .

The Memory of War and Children in Exile: (Poems 1968–83) James Fenton

'James Fenton is a poet I find myself again and again wanting to praise' – *Listener*. 'His assemblages bring with them tragedy, comedy, love of the world's variety, and the sadness of its moral blight' – *Observer*

The Bloody Chamber Angela Carter

In tales that glitter and haunt – strange nuggets from a writer whose wayward pen spills forth stylish, erotic, nightmarish jewels of prose – the old fairy stories live and breathe again, subtly altered, subtly changed.

Cannibalism and the Common Law A. W. Brian Simpson

In 1884 Tod Dudley and Edwin Stephens were sentenced to death for killing their shipmate in order to eat him. A. W. Brian Simpson unfolds the story of this macabre case in 'a marvellous rangy, atmospheric, complicated book . . . an irresistible blend of sensation and scholarship' – Jonathan Raban in the *Sunday Times*

FOR THE BEST IN PAPERBACKS, LOOK FOR THE 🐧

PENGUIN BOOKS OF POETRY

American Verse
Ballads
British Poetry Since 1945
Caribbean Verse
A Choice of Comic and Curious Verse
Contemporary American Poetry
Contemporary British Poetry
Eighteenth-Century Verse
Elizabethan Verse
English Poetry 1918–60
English Romantic Verse
English Verse
First World War Poetry
Georgian Poetry
Irish Verse
Light Verse
London in Verse
Love Poetry
The Metaphysical Poets
Modern African Poetry
Modern Arab Poetry
New Poetry
Poems of Science
Poetry of the Thirties
Post-War Russian Poetry
Spanish Civil War Verse
Unrespectable Verse
Urdu Poetry
Victorian Verse
Women Poets

PENGUIN INTERNATIONAL POETS

Anna Akhmatova   Translated by D. M. Thomas

Anna Akhmatova is not only Russia's finest woman poet but perhaps the finest in the history of Western Culture.

Fernando Pessoa

'I have sought for his shade in those Edwardian cafés in Lisbon which he haunted, for he was Lisbon's Cavafy or Verlaine' – Cyril Connolly in the *Sunday Times*

Yehuda Amichai   Translated by Chana Bloch and Stephen Mitchell

'A truly major poet . . . there's a depth, breadth and weighty momentum in these subtle and delicate poems of his' – Ted Hughes

Czeslaw Milosz

Czeslaw Milosz received the Nobel Prize for Literature in 1980. 'One of the greatest poets of our time, perhaps the greatest' – Joseph Brodsky

To Urania   Joseph Brodsky
Winner of the 1987 Nobel Prize for Literature

Exiled from the Soviet Union in 1972, Joseph Brodsky has been universally acclaimed as the most talented Russian poet of his generation.

Philippe Jaccottet

This volume, contains the first translations into English of the poetry of Philippe Jaccottet, 'one of the finest European poets of the century'.

Osip Mandelstam   Translated by Clarence Brown and W. S. Merwin

Like his friends Pasternak and Akhmatova, Mandelstam, through his work, bore witness to the plight of Russia under Stalin – for which he paid with his life.

Pablo Neruda

From the poet-explorer of his early years to the poet-historian of 'my thin country', Neruda's personal turning point came when he was posted to Barcelona as Chilean consul just before the Spanish Civil War.

PENGUIN LITERARY BIOGRAPHIES